A RAINBOW OVER THE RIVER

EXPERIENCES OF LIFE, DEATH AND OTHER WORLDS

Veronika van Duin

CLAIRVIEW

Clairview Books
An imprint of Temple Lodge Publishing
Hillside House, The Square
Forest Row, East Sussex
RH18 5ES

www.clairviewbooks.com

Published by Clairview 2003

A catalogue record for this book is available from the British Library

ISBN 1 902636 47 3

Cover by Andrew Morgan Design
Typeset by DP Photosetting, Aylesbury, Bucks.
Printed and bound by Cromwell Press Limited, Trowbridge, Wilts.

Dedicated to my Mother,
Barbara Lipsker, MBE

Acknowledgements

I would like to thank Siobhán Porter, Rachel van Duin, Mary and Mervyn Roulston, and Joy Davey, for reading and correcting the manuscript and encouraging me.
My very special gratitude goes to Jens Holbek, who gave me the confidence to write down what I saw and heard.

Contents

Preface

Last year my mother died. The time leading up to her death was an extraordinary period in my life, both in an outer and an inner sense. It was as though, in an outer sense, the life she had given me, the standards and concepts, customs and behaviour that she set down throughout my childhood all began to fall into place as sensible and practical ways by which to live. I felt, as I bathed, dressed, fed and cared for her, that I was beginning to understand the practical side of devotion. This was an attitude she had tried to drum into me, and which, being a naughty little girl and a stroppy adolescent, I had heartily resisted. Even as a middle-aged adult, I sometimes found her disciplined approach to life rather demanding.

In an inner sense, she took me with her on her journey towards the other side, which we who live on this side of the river call death. I was able to go over the river, on so many occasions, to see, witness and hear what the beings whom we call angels have to say to us mortals here on earth, and how they gently guide us when we reach a new state of consciousness after we have died.

The preparation for these experiences started much earlier in my life. It began with significant dreams, an urge to find appropriate meditations, and a challenging call from a little girl who died violently in Cambodia. Her demand upon me to help her cross the river of death, which reached my soul though I had never met her here on earth, woke me up to the reality of the other side.

Though often very frightened and unsure of myself, there was never a doubt in my mind as to the validity of the subsequent spiritual experiences that came to me over the years. And as time passed, I found corroboration of the steps I was taking on the path to real knowledge of the other side — through the work of Rudolf Steiner, the mystical tract *The Chymical Wedding of Christian Rosenkreutz*, and numerous other biographical witness accounts of the spiritual world.

After my mother died, I was asked to write down what I had seen and heard. There are many people who go through similar experiences, and perhaps they would be happy to know they are not alone in their encounters with spiritual beings. The other side overlaps our earthly life, is present simultaneously. We, however, often only find it when the barriers are down at moments of close encounter with death, or birth.

I chose to write this book in three parts. The first part deals with the path I took to spiritual seeing, in which I have tried to write truthfully of the spiritual events that wove into my ordinary life. The second part is a diary of my mother's dying, in which amidst the nitty-gritty of caring and cleaning, the other side opened its beauty and certainty to my inner vision. In the third part, I have recounted how I learned to understand the meaning of the world of the spirit, and the lessons to be learned from beings whose love shines over us from across the river that divides this world from the other side.

Veronika van Duin
Ireland 2003

Part One

THE OTHER SIDE

The other side burst through into my ordinary world on the wings of the strident screaming of a young child. My hair felt pulled, the soft fluff on the back of my neck bristled. My skin felt scratched, my stomach clenched and heaved with nausea. My eyes blurred in double vision, with the sight of this world and the seeing of another. I thought I was going mad.

To describe the other side is nearly impossible. Imagine that you are sitting in a comfortable chair in your sitting-room, hearing the birds singing outside your window, the cars passing in the distance, someone doing the dishes in the kitchen and the feel of your home, your family, your children and the neighbours next door a familiar reassurance. And at the same time, simultaneously, you are standing in another place, seeing another scene, hearing other sounds, another voice, another group of souls moving around you. Sometimes, even another form of life-beings, beings of light move around you and communicate, clearly and precisely but without words. You are yourself with your normal understanding and intellect, but at the same moment the other is also you, and you are inside them. Meaning communicates within you and within the other beings as water flows together where two streams meet. I can only describe it as a completely harmonious, disorientating and perfectly normal sensation all at the same time. One feels tilted yet upright, knowing yet unknowing, conscious yet confused. The experience is unnerving, frightening and yet oddly safe. One *knows* one lives in this world as well as in the other, that the other side exists. Nevertheless, the other side seems like a waking dream, tangible, real and vibrant as dreams can never be. Both sides—this ordinary life experience, and the other more alive, brighter and broader life experience—are convergent, mutually existent.

It feels very strange to talk about the other side. Finding the words to give it the reality it deserves—so that people who have not yet woken up to its presence can see it in their mind's eye—whilst also obeying the laws of truth, presents me with a real challenge. For years I told almost no one about these visits. They seemed even to me who experienced their reality, journeys not to be divulged for everyone's scrutiny. Today, I still feel uncomfortable, now more with a sense of overwhelming responsibility than with fear of my supposed madness or of being ridiculed. I am now ready to talk about the precious and reaffirming certainty of life beyond life, for other people to share in this joy, though I know some people will find it strange and unbelievable. Nevertheless, the other side is as real and close as making a telephone call to South Africa from Ireland.

Before I had visited South Africa, phoning from Ireland made my hands sweat and my breath come short because I would be speaking to someone on the other side of the world and I could not picture that person's very different environment. My son went to South Africa, and I missed him as though I might not see him again. He felt so out of touch, so distant and so lost to me. When I called him up and we talked, I felt rich with pleasure and pained with the deprivation of being unable to actually share his wonderful experiences in that strange land.

Then I visited South Africa. I saw the glories of brown, gold and orange tints that make that vast country so very special. I met the openness and warmth of its people and my connection to my son deepened in shared knowledge. Now when I telephone to South Africa, I can picture all its beauty, its pain and even smell the remembered smells. It has become real, and distance makes no difference any more.

This is exactly how it is with my visits to the other side. At first it was shocking, frightening and strange. I didn't know that one could go there so easily. I always used to imagine that one had to be a great saint, a holy person, a clairvoyant or just a bit mad to see life beyond life. But that I, ordinary me, aged 26 years, a wife and mother of three children (the last just six weeks old), should be able to travel across did not fit with the image of a holy gifted person. Believe me, I am very ordinary indeed—I have a quick temper, I talk too much, I like to have things my way, and I am very impatient. At that age, I did not yet even really meditate. I flirted with the idea, thought I might take it up some day, but what 'it' was I couldn't have described. I thought meditating might be going into a trance, which scared me and did not really attract my down-to-earth attitude to daily life.

Yet now, and throughout the next few days and nights, there was this screaming, distressed voice around me, tugging at my arms with broken sharp nails, wild eyed in panic and screaming, screaming, screaming! I tried to shake it off, telling myself that it was my imagination, but I could not focus myself on my everyday chores. I had my children to care for, meals to cook, a household to manage and, though I went on doing all those things, my inner self was entirely wrapped up in the other side, and the insistent screams that filled my being. The voice kept on screaming, high-pitched, totally consuming my awareness. The distress was so demanding that I wanted to do whatever the wild sound wanted me to do, in order to stop it. But I didn't know what it wanted! I should say what *she* wanted, because now I 'saw' that the voice came from a little oriental girl, perhaps three years old. She was pulling at my arm, hair tangled in wild motion, her mouth stretched wide in fear, her eyes squeezed shut.

From the first hearing to the seeing of the little girl took no actual earthly time at all. I was still sitting after lunch, my children sleeping their afternoon nap, and my baby also asleep. I was in our sitting-room, reading a book. But the awareness of her dire need continued, and I went through the rest of that day living in two worlds – the here and now of a young mother's life, and the here and now of a frantic, damaged oriental child. The evening brought no relief, neither did the night. In my sleep the screaming continued. I walked in a hot wet place of high trees and heard the banging sound of guns.

The morning was confusing, getting children up, feeding the baby, producing meals for my family. I wondered why no one noticed that I wasn't really in the house, in the kitchen, at all. I was standing in a village of huts, in the steamy forest, listening to gunfire and a screaming child.

After lunch, I sat down with the newspaper and opened it in the middle. There, standing in blind, mouth-stretching panic was the oriental child of my inner vision, in the village that formed my inner landscape. Instantly, as I gazed in shock at the photograph, the screaming stopped. The relief was so enormous that I could *feel* every breath that I took flowing smoothly in and out of my lungs. I read the article. A little child, the journalist reported dispassionately, had been taken for sport by soldiers in Cambodia. The journalist had taken her picture as she was running screaming from the noise of the gunfire. He too had run, but returning the next day, was told how these men had played catch with her, then for a joke and with laughter, had torn her in pieces, arms and legs wrenched from her little torso. They shot her mother after raping her, gunned down the rest of the villagers, those they had not tortured to death, and left the huts in flames. He had got this story from a wounded ancient who crawled out from his hiding place to tell of his horror.

I stared and stared at the photo, bile rising up in my mouth.

But the child, I reasoned, had gone, was dead, released from suffering. The silence was so loud that it hurt. And the release of tension made my muscles tremble. I thought that would be the end of it, that I had simply, for no reason that I could find, been transported to Cambodia in soul-sympathy with the troubled times. I could quite well believe this. I had always thought that people could *feel with each other*, so, with a strong imagination, why could one not feel with someone unknown on the other side of the world?

It was not, however, the end. The screaming started again, as soon as I sat down to breast-feed the baby, and my milk would not flow. So I had a baby screaming here on this side too! That night I could not sleep for the sound, the feel of the scratching little hand on my arm. I became quite distressed too, tossing and turning in shared agony. I thought I ought to tell my husband what was happening to me, but I didn't know how to say what filled my inner eye and ear.

So the next day I struggled to fulfil my daily chores and made an appointment to see the priest. He was an older man, a little odd but he had an open heart and mind. We had known each other for a long time so I felt he could be trusted to listen and to advise me.

I had absolutely no experience or reference for dealing with the child's need. I simply wondered if there might be some connection between me and the little girl from a past life. In my early adolescence I had come across Joan Grant's books. I found them fascinating and read them all, finding a special relationship to her far memories of Egypt. The book I liked the least was entitled *Return to Elysium*. I could not connect to these accounts of Greece, set in another world above that of the earth, finding the story alien and perhaps invented. It did not tie in with my personal picture of life after death. Her memories of the Native Americans were delightful and exciting, reading like a true adventure. But her lives in Egypt rang a bell, and I could connect to this particular concept of reincarnation as though I already knew all about it.

I walked across the road to talk to the priest, hearing the screaming continuously. He listened as I told him what was happening in and around me. I asked him if this was somehow connected to reincarnation. He did not answer me as I expected he might. He asked how old my baby was. Then he smiled, and said that the child in Cambodia had found an ear in me because I was still open to the world from whence we come through the birth of my baby. He said that she needed my help. He said that she could not go into the light without being made whole again. Then he asked me if I could go back to the village. I felt quite surprised. I had never left it since the screaming started. I was living in two places at once.

He told me to go back there deliberately, look for the place where the killing had happened and find the pieces of her body, put them together as in life and make her whole again. Then, he said, I should dig a hole and bury her. I should do all this, he said, with great love, devotion and no fear, nor should I hate the soldiers. They would find their own judgment. Then, he continued, I should stay to watch the little one walk into the light.

I had no idea how to do this. What he recommended would need a body, arms and legs. Would I have that on the other side?

That night, after feeding my baby, a bald-headed, sweet little boy, I lay in my bed next to my husband and let myself travel. Actually, that is such a bad description of what happened. I knew I was lying in bed, but simultaneously I was walking in the damp hot undergrowth, pushing my way against some unidentifiable resistance that dragged at my feet, always trying to put me back into bed at home. To say that I could smell the jungle is true and untrue because I couldn't smell it with my physical nose, but rather with another sense that *felt* the odour of decaying things. It was this sensation that weighed down my feet.

However, I walked straight to the spot where the child had died, the screaming and tugging leading me on. There was blood on the dark earth in splotches, and the soldiers were there, holding the little girl by her arms and legs and pulling her into pieces! Their laughter was terrible, grating and cruel. I could see them clearly, detailed, their uniforms dirty and irregular, bayonets stuck in their trouser legs, in pockets with straps. But I experienced my own person as being like a ghost, transparent and vague in outline. The best way to describe my sense of physicality is that it was like the Cheshire cat in the story of *Alice in Wonderland*, there and not there, fading into only a face or eyes, unless I concentrated on having the rest of my body present. I tried not to be afraid and knew myself to be getting clearer in outline. At the same time, I could see the little girl standing whole beside me, screaming, whilst her body was being quartered.

The less afraid I was, the more solid I became. I had wondered how I was going to collect her pieces when I was only a ghostly visitor. But now I knew that I could be solid enough as long as I believed in what I was doing. So I took her hand and together we collected the limbs, tender and sweet, and put them in their rightful places by her torso. I got a stick from the undergrowth and dug into the rotting ground, and buried the body, some inner instinct telling me to do this whilst singing a lullaby. The little girl watched me, becoming steadily more quiet. Then, once the burial ceremony was concluded, she walked away, her back to me, towards something that I could not see. I prayed it would be to her angel.

I was once more in my bed, exhausted and weak as if after a storm of tears or a raging temper. I thought I ought to be covered in sweat from the effort of digging, but of course I was just lying in my bed. But I felt stiff, my feet stretched as far as they could, my knees rigid, my hands folded over my breasts. It was an effort to move my muscles. The bliss was the healing silence all around me, the sound of my husband's breath, the little snuffle of my baby and the patter of the rain on the window. The girl from Cambodia had gone into the light. Though I did not see its brightness or colour, I knew that she was safe and at peace.

But I was very shaken by this experience and did not want to read the newspaper for some years. I was also puzzled as to why she came to me. What connection did I have with Cambodia? How did she choose me? Would it happen again? Was it just a one-off? Was I perhaps actually a bit mad? My husband seemed to have noticed nothing strange about me. I asked him if I had been weird during the last few days and he was surprised by my question!

My Spiritual Upbringing

Though not a religious person and with the usual arrogance of youth, I had grown up in a family that lived according to the teaching of Rudolf Steiner. This great philosopher and visionary had lectured and taught in Middle Europe at the beginning of the twentieth century, holding courses and seminars on just about every subject, but especially on social renewal. He formulated a new approach to education, created new art-forms, influenced modern medicine, agriculture and science. Most people who followed his teaching did so because they were drawn to his enlightened attitude towards the spirit, which he termed 'spiritual science'. His insights and knowledge of life beyond life, of what he called 'the spiritual world across the threshold', opened up new vistas in the materialistic world of the early twentieth century. He began his mystical teaching within the Theosophical Society, but branched out with his own following and formed the Anthroposophical Society in 1924. Growing up with parents whose essential outlook was formed by Rudolf Steiner's thinking could not but influence me. However, the philosophy was never forced upon me, nor was I reproached when I grew older and rejected my parents' beliefs. Essential to Steiner's teaching was the dictum that human beings should be free to think their own thoughts. The reality of the spirit demands freedom.

I had always known my angel, a guardian who watched over me. Not that I paid her much attention, unless I was in trouble with fear or anger. Then I sometimes felt her presence more powerfully and consciously. But as a child, I simply accepted the reality of guidance and protection. I never saw her, but I knew she was there all the time.

My parents told us, by means of stories when we were very young, how in former times, human beings saw spiritual beings behind every living created thing. The myths and legends of gods and goddesses, fairy-tales and stories demonstrated that once upon a time, human beings and spirits spoke to each other. I grew up in a world where the Creator Being made the world in seven days — days being symbolic of aeons of time — and that humanity was the last and greatest creation by God, in his own image. This meant to my childish mind that we could also be like God one day, if we were holy and good enough, and that we would all find a new Paradise one day, once we would truly understand how God and human beings are one, father and son, mother, brother and sister.

Elves, dwarfs and fairies peopled my childish world. As I grew older, I lost sight of them, and enjoyed the 'real' world very much. But an upbringing such as I had had caused me to ask questions. Now, because I was growing up and not a little child any more, my parents — my father in particular — explained the myths, the spirits behind matter, in a different way. He told me about angels, archangels, nine hierarchies of angelic beings who work to take evolution forward towards redemption, of sub-human retarding beings whose work is to make humanity non-human, non-thinking machine-like creatures, and that inasmuch as God existed so did the Devil. My teenage ears heard these things and my teenage mind scoffed at them. Such ideas! You had to be a bit daft and romantically imaginative to believe all that stuff, I thought, and argued as all adolescents do, with my 'out-of-date' parents. But my father simply said that the world had to evolve from somewhere and something. It was not logical that it arrived out of nothing. And that being so, who created the something? I could not get my head around these thoughts and so left it at that.

But in the back of my mind a feeling continued that behind matter there had to be a guiding principle. Science never quite answered my questions. It was simply too pat for me, to talk about molecules, atoms, etc. Who made them? Besides, I knew without a shadow of doubt that beings existed around and outside me. Whenever I felt in real trouble, moral difficulties, emotional mires, I could ask my angel and a resolution would well up in me. I would know how to go forward once more. When I became an adult, I spoke of this to my parents, and they told me to read Steiner. I would be able to learn how to *know* the spiritual world. We no longer needed to blindly believe, they said. We could, as modern human beings, learn to see and think and understand the world of the spirit. This was a bit much for me at the time. I did not want to read Steiner. I wanted to be an ordinary worldly person. So I put it all aside and did not think about it very often, the exception being when I was in trouble — and then the warmth of my angel would surround me, if I asked for help.

As part of my upbringing, I went to services in the Christian Community, an independent Christian Church. But once I turned 13, I was asked if I wished to be confirmed. This was not something I desired. I found priests and the institution of the Church a difficult thing. If we were all made in the image of God, how come some were more qualified to spread his word than others? And who ordained — authorized — these people to do so? It certainly wasn't God, or a spirit! It was just another human being. So what gave the priest the right to pull me into a church? He was really only another man, after all. So I refused, and no one forced me to reconsider.

But I liked the priest. He was an open-minded, cheerful, down-to-earth humorous man, and I respected him even though he was a priest. He was entirely real and not given to airy-fairy language or actions. He did not laugh on the occasion when I told him about knowing my angel. He was also not in the slightest bit patronizing when I described, in a rather defiant tone, my experiences of warmth and of understanding solutions after talking to my angel. I told him these things because I wanted to prove that he did not have a monopoly on spiritual things just because he was a priest! He listened and said that what I felt was not at all uncommon. I have since found this to be quite true. Many people feel or talk to, or see, or contact their angel, though they may call it by very different names. This encouraged me to talk to the angels of my children as they arrived, one after the other, into my life.

When I had become an adult, a mother and a wife, my friend the priest once said to me that I would never get on with my angel as I should until I had found a bit of humbleness. He said that I had no humility. This made me absolutely furious. What did humility have to do with knowing about the spiritual world and its beings? Either it was true that through spiritual science one could learn of the spiritual world, or it was not true and one would have to go back to blind belief. My religious life gained nothing from his statement, but my angel did not go away, and my children's angels worked with me to keep them well and safe. I always knew that I would know where my children were and whether they were in any danger. I was *told*, by that inner, yet all-embracing voice by which the angels identify themselves to me.

Guardian Angels

From my parents I had absorbed the idea that guardian angels are the nearest spiritual beings to us humans. We know them so well that we paint them, talk about them and think about them as though they look like us, except that they have wings and can fly. And they can be saviours for us in times of real need. However, we also all know that they don't respond well to bribery. Prayers have to have real meaning and contain real need. And the answers come in so many guises that we have to learn to read the riddles. It is our failure to do so which makes us think that prayers can go unanswered. Moreover, in my experience, angels don't understand material wants very well. Physical things are as invisible to them as their light is so often invisible to us. The other side is a *living* world, obeying absolute laws governed by pure creativity, unsullied by selfish wants and desires. The angels do what they are given to do, regardless of likes and dislikes. They don't have the personal feelings that we so often suffer, here on this side. So the answers to our prayers will come in ways that seem to make us more uncomfortable rather than less so! That is, if our prayers are not pure in spirit.

Apart from knowing my own angel, whom I took for granted, my first real and conscious contact with another angel was with the guardian angel of my eldest daughter. I saw her sometimes around the cradle, but mostly I felt her as a being of warmth and light.

I think it is necessary to explain why I use words like 'see' and 'hear' when trying to describe spiritual beings or the other side.

The sensation is like seeing and hearing, though it happens inside me. But it also happens outside my person, as though I have travelled a great distance and look back on myself from the other side of the world, sitting here in a chair. This is so impossible to explain that the easiest way is to use ordinary language. In this way, the other side can be 'painted' for those who have not yet been there consciously.

My daughter's angel is very upright, with bright warmth that embraces her. I had such trust in her power that I knew my little girl would be safe, even though deafness and autism trapped her awareness and limited her communication skills. When she was a little toddler, I confidently let her play, inside and outside, relying on her angel to tell me if she needed help. I was always told. Once, when she had been out too long, at the age of three years, I went looking for her and walked straight to the farm. It was after working hours and no one was there. I could hear a cow gently lowing in the barn. I went in and the farmer came round the corner to stop me because, he said, the cow had calved half an hour ago, and she would possibly attack me. I told him my daughter was inside. He looked shocked, and we went in quietly. There stood the cow, head lowered, tongue working briskly to clean and warm her calf as well as my daughter, who was happily sitting in the muck, stroking the newborn calf. The mother cow was not happy to let the little girl go, showing us her horns and bellowing. And all around was such a spread of warmth, not simply because cows give great heat. The warmth was inside us, around us and coloured a glowing red.

We had occasion to be very, very grateful to her angel when on holiday in Holland. As is well known, Holland is flat and there are no hills — except for where we were staying. We had gone out cycling, my husband, myself and our three children. And of course we found the one and only hill! Once at the top, the road sneaked down to the busy main road at the foot. What fun to go as fast as possible! We tried to stay together, calling to the children, two of whom instantly responded, but the eldest ped- alled merrily on, not hearing us. She moved so quickly out of reach that, though we rode like mad, she was too far gone. It was a narrow road, with no passing places, and on one side rows of cars were parked. Up this hill drove a tanker, and down flew my little deaf daughter. There was no way they could pass each other — and if they did, she would career right out into the busy road at the bottom. I stopped my bike and called out loud for help. I actually screamed, stretching my consciousness out as far as I could, and simultaneously feeling that this concentration of widening perception was also centring me into a point the size of a pea.

The lorry and the child passed each other at the only possible place, a gap between two parked cars.

I could no longer see her behind the truck, and the driver waved and smiled cheerfully as he went by. Then I could see again. My daughter had stopped and was holding her bike at the edge of the busy road. Over her seemed to shimmer a huge bright being. Then it was gone. I realized that I had called to her angel in a blind panic, not having enough confidence in this awful situation to talk quietly to her. I felt empty and wrong, sorry for my lack of faith in the extreme tension of the moment — and also a bit foolish for screaming so loudly in public. The great joy of seeing the angel was something I took time to contemplate only later, and then I wondered if I had imagined it. The warmth of inner confidence, however, stayed with me for much longer than the sighting.

One can appear to be either heartless or very stupid to other people when one enters into a mutual pact of responsibility with the guardian angels of one's children. I trusted them absolutely and let my eldest daughter experience the world without hovering over her, trusting also the angels of my two younger children. We worked together. Certainly, on the occasion that my daughter was knocked off her bike the driver of the car that hit her needed more comfort than she did. He did not think that my faith was of much use! However, she was quite unharmed and learned from this experience to look out for road traffic. But he was very angry with me for letting a deaf child loose on the road, though it was a cul-de-sac. He did agree that he should have been more careful, and that short of locking her in or putting a big sign on her back saying 'I AM DEAF' we would have to rely on angelic intervention! He left the house after a calming cup of tea, still muttering that I was relying on a figment of my imagination.

It was the building site foreman who shouted at me, the time she walked happily up a ladder and on to the roof beams of a half-finished village hall, because I had told him she would be quite safe. He wanted me to call her down. I explained that she was deaf and that she would come down by herself. But he insisted that I got her down. I went with him, and saw her playing on the pointed bit where the roof beams meet. I must admit I was a bit scared, it was so high up. I told him to climb the ladder and wave to her, smiling. He did this, and she looked at him, stood up, held up her hand as though grasping the hand of another, and walked down the sloping beam to the foreman on the ladder as though along a smooth broad path. He was as white as a sheet when he brought her to me and she was as happy and rosy as an apple. But the man had stopped shouting. He had seen her holding the hand of someone.

My eldest daughter has always needed her angel. And without fail her angel arranges things, so much so that now, in her adult life, when her handicaps could be such a stumbling block for her, I do not worry. The right people and the right circumstances always turn up and she learns and manages herself well in daily life. She has become a skilled potter and paints remarkably mature and original paintings. People who meet her are touched by her warmth and do not find it difficult to make contact with her, though she can only communicate through a limited sign language. Behind her stands her bright warm angel.

The angel of my second daughter is very different. She is silvery and musical and dependable. I used to let my children sleep outside in the pram when they were very small, and as we lived in the country it was quite all right to do this. But even in the country there are hazards. One afternoon I saw a few bees buzzing around her pram. When I went to look, she was fast asleep and under the pram hood a queen bee had gathered her grape-cluster of workers. They hung quietly above the sleeping baby's head.

I knew she would be quite safe. That is, my inner self knew this, but my outer self was not so sure. I felt that God helps him who helps himself. We are not supposed to take angels for granted, and if the angel had led me to see the bees then I would need to find a way to remove them. Being practical is not a denigration of the spiritual world! I fetched the bee-keeper from next door and he collected them in his net without my daughter even stirring. The silvery light had been so constant that I didn't worry at all. I still put her out to sleep but I did put a net over the pram hood. The guardian angel's might should not be abused, I think.

The angel who guards my son is powerful and unapproachable. I have always felt in awe of him. He watches over him and talks to him directly. He has always dealt out consequences instantly and my son called them 'God-deeds' as soon as he could talk. Whenever he stepped out of line, he would receive a reminder, such as hurting himself or dropping his toy, or some other small consciousness raiser. He understood their meaning from when he was very small and still lisped. He would come with a scraped knee and say through his tears: 'It wath a God-deed, Mummy, becauthe I teathed my thithter!'

Later, as he grew up, we sometimes communicated through his angel. I had made it a conscious habit to speak to my children's angels before going to sleep, and when they were adults I still went on doing it. I always knew how they were and, more often than not, knew which one was at the other end of the telephone line before I lifted the receiver. With my daughters, the communication was easy and smooth, telling me little things like their health and their state of mind. With my son, it was of decisions, confrontations and inner turmoil. On one occasion, when he got mugged in Johannesburg, I knew before the phone rang. I had a tremendous headache and felt dizzy with anxiety.

After this happening, I decided to pray openly and directly to his angel. By this I do not mean that I prayed out loud, but I made an inner effort to ask his angel to stand over him as protection against the darkness in the world around him. Then the phone rang, from somewhere in Africa: 'Mother, please stop it. I can't sleep any more. You're taking away my freedom, and I have to live my own life. I can *hear* your prayers!'

Clinging onto someone so strongly through their angel is quite possible, but not very forgivable. So I stopped, and we went back to the usual conscious concern. But then he made his choice of a career – he joined the military. He had always said one day he would fly aeroplanes. I realized that it was not my place to interfere. Bringing one's children up to become free individuals will always hold the risk that what they do and think may not be along the lines you might want them to do and think. So outwardly I accepted his path, but inwardly I struggled for real acceptance. I tried to address his angel and experienced a barrier, high, wide and deep, as though he spoke: 'No more. Beyond this you may not walk.'

I felt shattered and also reproved. Would we find nothing more in common? The loneliness hurt. I couldn't talk to his angel any more. However, the next time I met my son I was deeply impressed by his uprightness and confidence. I did, it is true, feel on the outside, knowing I could not understand his life's mission fully. I also felt very ashamed of my fear on his behalf.

I know he has chosen his destiny and trust in him, his judgements and his understanding of truth. He has become *himself*. I do not try to talk to his angel any more. Sometimes he approaches me, powerful and huge, but in some odd way reassuring too.

Music of the Spheres

Talking to my angel and those of my children was not quite the only contact I had had with the other side before the eruption of the little girl. When I was 16, I entered into a phase of deep unhappiness with myself, my life and my ideals. Though outwardly things were fine, I was happy at school, loved my home, had many friends and read voraciously, wanting to know everything I could possible learn to know, my inner aims were unclear and I felt I did not really know who I was or where I was going. And then I travelled one night into another space and time.

There was no darkness, only light. This is not a true description, because the light of the 'sky' was actually a kind of blue that was so deep it had gone beyond darkness and become light again. And in that shimmering background twinkled millions upon millions of stars. As I rose up into the sparkling lights they moved into a three-dimensional spiral and showed their colours. They whirled into enormity, each star-colour filling the whole of space yet always giving way to another star-colour's light. Their light was shaded into all the hues that ever existed.

These colours were brighter than any I have seen in the light of day, except when seeing the after-image of a colour in our physics lesson at school. We had to experiment with the magic of the eye, that it creates its own light with which it can see. You look at a colour, for example blue, without blinking, then transfer your gaze to a white sheet of paper. Instantly, shimmering and glowing, the colour of orange lights up on the white sheet, taking the exact shape of the blue circle painted on the other sheet. But the blue is flat and dead paint compared to the living orange complementary colour that the eye produces on the back of the blue dead paint. Such were the colours I now saw.

They shimmered and blended, one into the other, through the other, over and under the other, yet never lost their differentiation or singular identity. Myriad is too few to describe their number, a multitude not seen here in this world, and each colour resounded in a tone particular to itself. These tones harmonized into music that I cannot describe in words, but its beauty made me expand and grow and thin out with longing to join the coloured music and dance with the tones. They were moving in a form that held meaning, as though it were a kind of living writing. The harmony of the spheres that Shakespeare refers to must be something like the music I heard, and saw. The tones narrowed themselves into a meaningful formation and the meaning told me: 'Not yet. It is not the right time.' I pleaded with the manifold coloured sounds and as I pleaded, they danced into a closer and closer pattern that pushed me inside myself. I shrank into a tiny focus and found myself in bed, stretched out, arms folded over my breast, feet so cold and lifeless, muscles so stiff that I could hardly move. It was painful to find myself still alive. I wanted so much to return to the living vibrant colour and ringing tones of the other world.

The Discipline of Meditation

The experience of being a conveyor to the little girl was very sobering. The absolute power of it reminded me of the reality of the spiritual world, which the colours and music of the spheres had taught me ten years ago. I asked the priest for some guidance, perhaps he could recommend a meditation, and he helped me to find the path that suited me. From that time on, I mostly managed my meditation, not always as faithfully and completely as I aimed to do, but by and large I stuck to the path. And I did not want to cross over again. It had been as terrifying this time as the first time had been blissful. I did not want to be a bit strange in the head, and I wanted to understand how to control such experiences should they ever happen to me again. This was the reason to begin a path of meditation. Moreover, I had recently read Joan Grant's book called *Far Memory* in which she describes some part of how she trained herself to see clearly and remember accurately. She would test what she saw, and if she could shift the picture, or change details, then she knew it was only a dream. But if she could change nothing, no matter how hard she tried, she knew it to be a true memory picture. I decided that if ever I travelled across again, I would apply this technique.

Echoes of a Past Life

Not that I could, or even can, remember my past lives. But that I have lived before I do not doubt. It is a simple certainty inside me. Not so long ago I visited Rhodes. There are many ruined castles of the Knights of St John, an order linked to the Knights Templar. They were the world's bankers of the Middle Ages, amassing untold wealth and lands across the whole of Europe and the Middle East. On entering the city of Rhodes, I felt as though I would faint. Nausea choked me, my head began to pound and I thought I had sunstroke, despite wearing a sensible sun hat. My husband left me sitting by the roadside for a while, and when I felt a bit better I ventured up the street that lead to the castle of the Grand Master of the Order. The nearer I got to it, the more ill I felt. Inside the castle I could hardly control the urge to vomit. So we walked down and caught the bus home.

No sooner had we cleared the ancient town walls than I instantly recovered. The choking sensation, as if a rope were strangling me, had completely vanished. We laughed it off as something weird and wonderful. Then we saw, on another outing, a ruin on the hillside. We climbed up, stepped over the wall beside an old and disused well, and I fell down almost in a faint, struggling for breath, as though choking and drowning simultaneously. My husband dragged me over the wall, and instantly I could breathe again.

This time, we decided to test it out. I told him that I felt I was being strangled and drowned upside down in the well. Together we climbed over the wall, and this time I was expecting the terrible sensation. Though I wheezed and broke out into a sweat, I tried not to panic but simply to explore the awful feeling. It was exactly the same, but now I could hold it in place as an *other time* experience and not my actual in-this-life death. It was truly horrible, but interesting too.

When I got home, I asked someone who knew a great deal about history and did not laugh at the idea of reincarnation whether I could have been experiencing death in a past life. He told me something about the Knights of St John in Rhodes. He explained that if a member of the order betrayed a trust or revealed a hidden secret in connection with their initiation rites, or did not follow his vows, after sentencing, he would be taken to that particular castle on the hill and choked with a rope whilst being drowned upside down in the well. Whether this was a past-life experience or my picking up on the distress of somebody who had died in this terrible way, I cannot judge. But it made me think of Joan Grant's many remembered lives.

The Power of Evil

I did not find my way across to the other side again for many years. That is, not in a fully conscious sense. But when I was 33, I did, in a state between waking and sleeping, find a new understanding of the truth of Evil, as well as of the reality of reincarnation.

Evil came to my knowledge in full power when my children were still in nursery school. We lived at that time in Hertfordshire, in a lovely village with friendly inhabitants, and we were very happy indeed. Our family was close, we enjoyed each other and the warmth of the home. My husband was working as a lorry driver and I supplemented our income by working as a charwoman. I enjoyed it very much. I loved making things shine, polishing and tidying, which is, I know, a very unfashionable thing to which to admit! But I derived great satisfaction from the simple ordinary day-to-day activities of housekeeping, whether for my family or for someone else. I had few ambitions and just wanted to live life as it came along. Having three children is quite time consuming and I was always busy. And my husband enjoyed driving lorries. He was often away, doing runs to the Continent. Our three children were happy, too, the school they attended providing them with interests and friends. I too gained many friends through my children and was hardly ever lonely. Our neighbours couldn't have been better. Not being able to drive, and my husband so often absent, I could always find someone to help out with trips. We were rather poor, but the shopkeepers helped out too, letting me pay at the end of the week. I felt extremely fortunate to be living in such a warm and supportive environment. Life was good and very ordinary indeed. No highs and no lows.

Into this nest, as we lay sweetly sleeping, Evil intruded. This was the first time I consciously experienced myself to be in another place, whilst being in my own familiar home. I was able to be a witness to my own spiritual activity, an observer of the following events, whilst also being the protagonist. Therefore the appearance of evil had a definite *physical* place in which it made its stand, on a high hill. Planted on the top were three stone rectangular altars, the middle one a little bigger than the two that flanked it. To say these blocks were planted is quite accurate because I could see that they had roots that went deep into the mountain, so deep that I could not see their end. They were standing on the hill as though they were teeth in a jaw-bone. The sky behind them was dark and restless. From these altars emanated darkness.

This part is very difficult to describe in words because though darkness is correct it was not black and opaque, but streaming and vibrating as light is to our open eyes. But instead of revealing things to us, as light does, I saw that the running darkness obliterated things, wiped them out of existence.

I saw three beings flying from these altars to our house. Again, flying is a poor word, though correct, to explain the movements these beings made as they slid, crawled or slithered through the dead air. I saw them from my bed, through the walls of our house. Solid as the walls were, I could see through them. The beings were cloaked in flowing darkness, thicker than the streaming murk, and had human-like shapes but with heads, bodies and arms that were broader than human, almost wing-shaped. They did not appear to have legs. Their bodies faded into the general murkiness of the moving darkness. I knew that the three were making for my children. I also knew that I could not allow them to enter into the house, because they wanted to enter into the souls of my children. I was as frightened as I had ever been, with a fear so cold and paralysing that I could not move my limbs. But I knew that I must move, must make my way into the children's room. What I would do after that I did not know.

The odd thing about this seeing was that I was aware of lying in my own bed in the other room next door to my children, yet I could see through the wall into their room where they lay in their beds, and through the curtained window out towards the mountain – which I knew in waking reality was not really there at all. I was, just as had been the case when my daughter almost died on her bicycle in Holland, both stretched out to the horizon, and diminished to the innermost centre of my being.

I succeeded in getting to their room against a tide of fear that wanted to engulf me, wanted to push me back. I felt so cold and lifeless that I thought I would never manage the few steps I needed to take. (I was, throughout the experience, physically still lying in my bed, as was my husband.) Finally, I stood in the middle of the children's room, and saw that my husband had wandered in behind me, sleepwalking. I tried to wake him up, knowing that to be in this state made him terribly vulnerable to the awful beings. He would not wake. He slowly slipped down to his knees, then on all fours, then on his belly on the carpet between the children's beds. He drooled at the mouth and snorted peculiar sounds, pawing at my feet and legs as though trying to pull me down. I was filled with anxiety, overladen by compassion for his state of being, but I could not help him. If I were to help any of us, I would need all my strength to withstand the terrible figures that approached so frighteningly silently. Eventually, as I did not bend to him, he just lay there. I was now so afraid that I wanted to run, run anywhere to escape from here.

I saw the three beings, the central one with a cloak over his head and face, the two on either side with shapes for heads but no faces, only pockets for eyes. The place where the faces should have been was white, like a pale two-dimensional shadow, sickly and glowing. But the eye pockets were worse, raying out darkness as a lantern rays light. The dark rays were the means with which they could penetrate into any material thing and so follow in order to inhabit their chosen object. They searched for the children, not finding them as they slept peacefully in their beds, unconcerned within a cradle of bright light.

But they found me, and they found my husband, lying unconscious on the floor. I tried to outstare the glowing darkness, but my soul was so thin with the effort of remaining upright that I could not do it. I knew I would soon crumble, as my husband was flattened already. I needed help, support, courage, something onto which to hold, to cling. The shelter and protection around my children was for them alone. I knew that I had to find my own strength.

From somewhere deep within me a memory stirred, like a small song. A verse from the Old Testament filled my mind and so I tried to recite it, with stiff lips. As soon as I began, the central Evil raised its bowed, covered head and I saw its eyes through the covering, the dark rays from the eye pockets burning through the cowl. I thought I was blasted away, so I sang louder, my lips starting to move more freely. And I raised my hand to above my head where I could *see* a gleaming golden thread rising into eternity from my fontanelle. Whether the golden thread came from my head or began in eternity I do not know. But the Evil hated it, trying with its dark light to cut the cord. The other two writhed against the house, trying to push through the walls. The central figure grew and grew in proportion to the growing confidence in my voice. Then all three vanished. The altars on the hilltop began to sink, disappearing into the earth and my husband began to stir.

I found myself in my bed, my husband by my side. Once again I was lying cold, stiff, my hands crossed on my breast, and I ached with cold. I lay, waiting for warmth to fill my body and recited over and over again: 'I will lift up mine eyes unto the hills. My help comes from my Lord. He that keepeth me will not sleep.'

These were the words, no, rather the content of the words that had kept the Evil out. But that the beings were real, were present in the world and could do harm was a compelling truth within me.

After some time, I got up and checked my children. They slept peacefully and soundly. The hill in the distance was gone. So real had the hill been that I opened the curtains to check, though realizing that this was nonsense as it was pitch dark, in the early hours of a winter morning.

I thought a great deal about the thread of light from my head to eternity, or from eternity to my head. I think everyone has such a thread, a lifeline to the spirit, but knowing of it and finding it is the big secret in our time. The Evil does not want us to know it. Perhaps we can only really use it when confronted by the great lie that the dark rays from dead eye pockets show to us.

I know this was a real experience because of the position I found myself in on coming back to ordinary consciousness. It was the same as on the previous occasion, the posture of the physically dead or someone undergoing Egyptian initiation. By now I dreaded another such experience. I felt quite unequal to it, not knowing what I should do with such knowledge. So I decided to keep it to myself. I did not want to be thought odd, or that people should laugh at the truth.

Some weeks after this terrible confrontation, we went on a Sunday outing. We often drove out at weekends to explore the area around us, enjoying the lovely countryside. And so we took a turning to High Wycombe. As we drove over the hill and looked down its steep incline to the town below and saw the road's rise up the other hillside, I realized it was the mountain I had seen in that awful night. I said nothing to my family, but sat stunned and fearful in my comfortable front seat of our Ford Cortina. We drove on and up the hill, stopping at a sign that indicated a pavilion or temple. My husband wanted to go inside, but I could not bear to do so having read the description in the brochure that we picked up at the entrance, which described what its function had been some centuries ago. It had been a centre for a Satanic cult, whose rituals were carried out by means of sexual orgies, in which the perpetrators hoped to raise the Devil. I insisted we left at once, much to my husband's annoyance. The vision I still bore of those terrible beings was too close for comfort and I did not want my children to be in their vicinity a moment longer.

I had learned something that I never forgot – that Evil works primarily on earth. It works through human beings who do not raise their unconscious actions, thoughts and feelings into a real and wakeful awareness. It is dreadfully dangerous to sleep away one's life. One lays oneself bare to become tools of the forces of Evil.

When I had almost completed the manuscript for this book, I gave it to my daughter to read. She came back to me with it in her hands, and said that she recognized the three evil beings. She had suffered from terrible nightmares whilst we were living in Hertfordshire. She would almost wake up and see the three dark beings trying to get into her room. So afraid was she that she would scream, and thankfully I would always come to comfort her. But the worst part of these attacks was the fact that the beings still remained, in the curtains and the clothing that hung in her room. They never quite left her. So she took a book of prayers that belonged to me, and put it under her pillow. I found that book and, thinking it unsuitably adult for a child of seven, offered her the christening gift from her godfather, a bible. This she gratefully put under her pillow, to hold on to when the beings attacked. From then on the dreadful creatures faded away. She had not been able to describe what she saw that made her so frightened because she could not find the words, but my giving her the bible had been a hugely comforting talisman. She said she had entirely forgotten this episode in her life until she read my manuscript.

The Reality of Reincarnation

Learning the reality of reincarnation came to me when I was 37. The years had passed and no more intrusions from the other side happened, nor did I try to cross over. I worked more regularly with meditation, but had begun to try prayer too. Praying is very different from meditating. I find that it asks of one to open up, make an offering, lay oneself bare to the greater good, accept one's weaknesses and offer them humbly to the angels. Meditating, on the other hand, asks one to focus, to concentrate, to enter consciously into a spiritual state, and I found it such hard work. Also, I was a little afraid that this effort might take me across and I felt so unprepared. Moreover, I had been frightened quite enough by now. I had a healthy respect for the powers of evil and I knew the great good that flowed through the angels of God. I chose to relate to these beings in prayer, but I did still battle on with meditation.

I moved with my family to live with people with disabilities, in a community. It was made up of people of all nationalities who chose to share their lives with the disabled. It is hard work, living with and caring for all types of disabilities. My children were getting on in school, we lived all together in an extended family and I was happy, busy, and studying spiritual science. Life was good, but in a very different way from my previous quiet, sub-urban activities. I still worked mainly at housekeeping, but now for up to 30 people of varying ages and abilities. My husband ran a workshop in the community, a general store that employed adults with disabilities, and so I saw a good deal more of him than before. My daily life included everyone in the community in one way or another. To create community, one needs good communication and organizational skills, so I attended a num-ber of weekly meetings concerning the daily running, the cul-tural life and the care and social needs with which disabled people require assistance. It was challenging, stimulating and often exasperating to work with such a variety of abilities and so many differing cultural backgrounds.

Community life is not always harmonious. One comes up against one's own nature a little too often and sometimes a little too painfully. And one comes up against the nature of other people. One cannot do things one's own way, and the way others do things can be abrasive and confrontational. All too often I asked myself why we had decided to live like this. The silly saying 'You don't have to be mad to work here, but it helps' seemed very appropriate a lot of the time. The only answer that gave me any satisfaction was that I *wanted* to do what I was doing. So, I reasoned, if I wanted to do this, then from where did my motivation come?

The ethos behind the community in which we lived was based, once again, on Rudolf Steiner. And his philosophy, as I understood it at that time, was built on the knowledge of reincarnation and karma. To live life properly, one must work on developing self-knowledge so that one can achieve one's true karmic aims brought with one from before birth. In the world of spirit before birth, one arranged things in such a manner that what one required in order to fulfil one's karma, one's destiny, would make themselves apparent throughout one's earth-life.

Given this thought it therefore followed, I reasoned, that I had chosen before being born to live and work with special needs people in a community. So, I continued with my self-convincing argument, there had to be some karmic connection between me and all the other people with whom I now lived. So why did I not love them all?

This was a really difficult question for me. I did truly want to love and accept everyone, but in the reality of daily life many people irritated me. I saw that I irritated them, and life was not at all a bowl of cherries!

We lived in a house with twelve children covering the spectrum of disabilities and challenging behaviour. Little children at the best of times can be trying, but the children in my house seemed often to dish out the most astonishing things. We were not unused to plates flying at meal times, to floodéd bathrooms and soiled bedrooms. But gradually, as we grew to know each other, and the young volunteers who joined us each year became more experienced, we blended into a very happy, albeit quite big family. My children joined in and the residents became their playmates. They were all young enough not to notice too many differences between able and disabled. In fact, the more able helped the less able as a matter of childish pride.

On one occasion, standing at the top of our stairs, I had watched my son walking up past a child of his own age who was walking down. They met on the turning, stopped and looked each other in the eye, then walked on, one up and one down. My son burst into tears and flung himself at me, beating my chest and shouting: 'Why can I talk and Jimmy can't talk?' And I found I did not have a satisfactory answer for him. Anything I could have said would have been quoting someone else's experience, not my own. I thought I understood that we come from somewhere before birth and go somewhere after death, but I did not *know* this except from my study of spiritual science. And I did not want to lie to a child. I wanted to answer him with real understanding, real authority. So I could only comfort him with hugs and kisses.

Coupled with all this soul-searching, I was physically in a poor state of health and could not sleep properly. I lay awake for the most part of every night, struggling to sleep, achieving at most a level of half-sleep that disorientates and leaves one more tired afterwards. I dreamed a great deal, stupid, unfulfilling ordinary dreams – except for one.

I stood with several other people in a large hall, the ceiling so high that I could not see it properly, and perhaps it wasn't there at all. The hall had twelve great arching windows, without glass, on three sides. The fourth side was a wall of books such as you see in the libraries of old palaces, the shelves going upwards into the high distant vague roof of the hall. I was present in this great castle together with many other people and we stood, backs to the windows, facing the book-lined wall. Though I had my back to the window, I could see that outside was a blue sky, clear like it is after rain, no clouds, and I knew it was very, very windy.

In the left-hand corner a secret door opened, unnoticed because it too was lined with books. A tall imposing figure entered, followed by two servants. The figure was cloaked in brown velvet and wore a strange hat, broad and climbing to a peak. It was made of some golden material, stiff, yet soft. And though I would call him a man, he had no sex, only the aura of maleness. The servants were sexless too, neither male nor female. The man was apparently our teacher. He approached each of us and asked us a question. I could not hear what he said to each person but I understood he was giving them a choice. Most of the other people vanished as soon as they had been spoken to. But two walked quietly through the secret door. Eventually he stood in front of me. He had penetrating eyes as he asked me my question. I still did not hear what he said though his lips moved, but I understood what he asked and I made my choice. I could either go out of the hall through the secret door, or go out altogether. 'Out there' was terrifying, but I knew I was not ready to go through the door. I wasn't far enough in my studies.

No sooner had I made my choice than I was hurled out backwards through the window behind me and somersaulted head-over-heels down a steep hillside, helter-skelter and without any control. I landed breathless and confused in a gutter. I lay, winded, gradually aware of my surroundings. The stink was appalling, pig-muck, human waste, rotting vegetables and rats scurrying. The noise was terrible too. Animals brayed, bellowed and clucked. It was a market-place, houses leaning crookedly over the square, drovers shouting and pedlars singing their wares. Children, ragged and half-dressed, scampered over me and a donkey almost stepped on me. I did not know where I was or what was happening to me. I knew I was in a market town in the fourteenth century, but my awareness was tuned to today's world, so I felt as though acting in a real life drama, set in the Middle Ages.

For fear of being trodden on, I rolled up against a house wall, still in the gutter, and just missed having a slop pot poured over me from a window above. People shouted and laughed in a language that I could not understand. Though the meaning was clear, the words were unfamiliar.

I saw that I was stark naked, and that I was a man. This amazed me. The sight of my sexual parts was strange enough but the feeling of them was even stranger. They got in my way and I was terrified of being looked at in my naked state, for all to see. So I curled up in a ball, and put my hands over myself, trying to get used to being male. A shrill feminine voice called to me over my head. It wanted to know my name. Another deeper voice answered her, soothing, oily, and threatening. It spoke in unfamiliar words, but the meaning was quite plain: 'Leave him alone. He doesn't yet know his name. It will come to him. He's only just arrived here from "up there".'

I uncurled myself in surprise, seeing a pointing finger stretched up to the hillside beyond the town. It looked distant and next door to me simultaneously. It was a green hill, rounded, and on the top, hazy and wavering, was the outline of a ruined Norman castle. I was extremely surprised and also very frightened. I had come from a great house, with arched ceilings and windows, beautiful, stately and cultured. The ruin I saw was crumbling, square and threatening, dead memories shuffling around it like ghosts. Only the blue sky and windswept clouds held an echo of the place from whence I had come.

Something in the deeper voice frightened me dreadfully. It knew what was up there, knew that I came from another place and time, and revelled in its power of knowing. I realized that it was very important that I would not tell these two where I came from. I would have to be the innocent that I was, and perhaps I would learn from them how to live in this strange place and alien time.

The feminine voice told me to get up. I looked at her and knew that she was the Whore, painted and perfumed, the stale stench of old passion emanating from her almost bared breasts. She was dressed in some yellow cloth, embroidered and stained. She had reddish hair curled up over her forehead and pale blue eyes. She held out a cloak to me, which I took to cover myself but not before she had looked me over with a smirk at my unclothed privates. It made me very uncomfortable to be wanted for my manhood. I still thought like a woman and I did not know how to react. But I did not want *her*.

Now I had time to see the other person. He was the Juggler. It was odd, but I seemed to have been expecting the two of them and recognized their names immediately. The Juggler was dressed in parti-coloured clothes, red and green, and had bells sewn on the points of his shoes. He wore a three-horned cap, also with bells at the tips, like the jesters of old. He was clean-shaven and had black snapping eyes and a permanent grin. But the eyes did not smile, and the lips held a sneer. I was extremely frightened of him.

They spoke to me in a very friendly way, promising that they could teach me all I needed to know to live well in this world. They took me to a tailor and got me some clothes – a grey shirt, a leather jerkin, brown leggings, a pair of long-toed shoes and a hat. I put them on, feeling the rough woollen hose against my bare skin. It was warm and protective and I did not feel so loose and uncomfortable any more.

Still friendly, they showed me the market, telling me what everything was as though I were an idiot. I could understand them very well, but I could not speak. By the evening, I knew I could now talk, but I did not want to. I thought I was safer without language. The Juggler decided we should eat, so we went to a tavern. It wasn't very clean. There were long scrubbed wooden tables with benches on either side and it was packed full with farmers and merchants of all sorts. It was loud, smelly and rough. I seemed to have been used to quiet meals, conversation hushed and intermittent, because I could not cope with the bustle and felt sick.

The Juggler got me a bowl of soup and half a chicken. I tried to eat the chicken but the smell made me want to vomit. I could get the soup down, a vegetable broth with cabbage floating in it. The Juggler nudged the Whore and whispered that 'none of them could eat meat. It comes from the training "up there".' The Whore sniggered and made sounds that seemed to say that she hoped it would not impair my performance later on.

It was then that I became aware that the Juggler planned for me to have sex with the Whore. I also realized that this was of vital importance to them both. They *needed* me to do this. They began to try to make me drunk. I sat on the bench, sandwiched between them whilst they poured out flagon after flagon of beer, consuming most of it themselves. The Whore tried to sit on my lap, urging herself upon me, but there was no space on the bench. Everyone around us was noisily drunk, fights were breaking out and I sat, trying not to drink the beer. But some of it went into me, forced down my throat by the Juggler, whose grin was still fixed on his face. His eyes bore into my soul, telling me that what I could have with the Whore would be untold bliss. But I was afraid, so afraid that I could not act at all.

Then they took me upstairs, into a bedroom. The floor-boards were bare, and the noise from downstairs came up through the cracks with the smell of old food and stale beer. I wanted to vomit again, but they tied me into a chair and began to try to force alcohol down me. It spilled over my shirt as I resisted, but some I swallowed and could feel all resistance fading. The Whore overwhelmed me, pushing herself onto me. She smelled terrible, of sweat and human grime and I gagged at this attention. The Juggler cursed, saying that if I would not lie with her they would kill me.

Somehow I understood that if I did what they wanted they would gain power over the Hall from where I had come. I would not give in. They got me up from the chair and forced me to lie on the bed. They stripped me of my hose, and the Whore began to try to rouse me. The sensation was horrible, rough and compelling. I shrivelled up into myself. The Juggler urged her on with lewd suggestions, meanwhile pouring more beer into me so that I had to drink. I choked but could not struggle very much, my legs and arms feeling horribly limp.

Eventually, the Juggler gave up. I was now so drunk that I could not move except to want to drop my head and go to sleep. They dragged me out by my arms, down the passage to a room at the back. They lifted the floor-boards and underneath I saw a coffin in the ground. I knew they would bury me alive. I could not struggle because of the alcohol and I knew that it had been a sin to drink even a drop. With the first mouthful, I had separated myself from my true teacher. But I had not been able to prevent the Juggler. He was stronger than I was.

Now they manhandled me into the coffin, the Whore crying because I had refused her, cursing and kicking me. The Juggler had lost his grin, and I knew that it was because he was furious that they had not succeeded in making me lie with the Whore. The importance of this act escaped me, but the union must have had great significance for them because all the while they were shoving my helpless body into the coffin they were cursing the failure, once again, of their mission, as though they had done this many times before. Then they placed the lid on, and I was in total darkness, waiting for earth to be thrown on top. It followed, thud, thud, thud, and I breathed less and less, feeling the trap of my body holding me fast in terror.

The darkness weighed on my eyelids as I struggled to open them. I was in my bed, stiffly outstretched, arms folded across my breasts. And I was so cold, I could not move a muscle. I was returning from near death. It took a while before I could open my eyes, could see the curtains on my window, could hear the breathing of my husband, could begin to move a bit.

I wanted desperately to let go of being alive. Being in my body was suffocating me. It felt exactly like the coffin into which I had just been pressed. It was a living death to have a physical body. But slowly warmth crept around me from my duvet and I realized that I was not a man at all. I was a woman again.

To describe the disorientation of my sex is extremely difficult. I suppose the best way would be to say that I knew who I was, but not *what* I was. I mentally explored my body, and felt bereft and relieved. Something I had not wanted was removed from me, but I also missed it.

Gradually, my legs and arms belonged to me again and I could sit up and look at the time. It was 3 o'clock in the morning. I was too worn out to get up, and I did not want to disturb my husband by switching on the lamp. However, I needed light, needed to see myself, my bed, my room, my husband. So I woke him up. He was, needless to say, not very pleased, and too grumpy to listen to a description of my experience. So I let him sleep and lay beside him, trying to arrive in my present world and make sense of the overpowering images.

The outcome of this strong experience was that I saw children and adults with disabilities in a very new light. I suffered their physical entrapment with them, especially those with autistic spectrum disorder. To be able to speak and understand and yet not be able to transpose this into words of one's own isolates beyond measure. People treat you as if you were either a genius or a fool. And they want something from you that you cannot give them.

To live in a physically disabled body is to be buried alive. All your faculties of feeling work overtime, and your limbs do not obey you.

To suffer from epilepsy means that your consciousness is over-filled with impressions until they burst out of you and you rise above to perceive the world from outside. Being *in* the world is to be over-conscious of yourself. This is often very painful and makes you want to scratch the people around you, physically and metaphorically speaking.

I saw all humanity as being trapped, being forced by their bodies to do things they might never, as their real selves, have actually wanted to do. And I wondered about the sexes. How different it is to be a man than a woman! A woman takes the world into herself, nurturing and fussing over everything. A man is too vulnerable to absorb. He needs to stride out and repel the world in order to protect his sensitive self. I suddenly seemed to understand why disabilities appear more often in the male body. It is much weaker than the female, and much more open to persuasion.

Why the Juggler found it so important for me to have sex with the Whore I could not understand. I just had to accept that the sexual act in spiritual terms means more than we think it does when we live in our physical bodies. But I was extremely glad to be a woman in this life.

Many years later, I came across *The Chymical Wedding of Christan Rosenkreutz*. I read it with excitement and relief, at last gaining a little understanding of the extraordinary experience with the Juggler and the Whore. Christian Rosenkreutz travelled much farther than I did, but he too describes similar experiences, though he does not go into any detail. He merely hints at the aspect of the sexes, and one has to enter into his story to find the answers. But I suddenly grasped what was shown to me through the actions of the Whore. The female breast represents cosmic food. If this is perverted, it becomes food that satiates our lowest nature. Male sexuality represents the ultimate human power of creation, and if it is perverted it becomes power for destruction. Male and female both are filled with the potential of true creator might — but if we fall into the hands of the Whore and the Juggler, we fail in our God-given task.

I also understood why I chose to leave the Hall, and why I was not yet far enough in my studies. Obviously I still needed the lessons taught to me by the Juggler and the Whore.

Encounter with a Stranger's Past Life

To work with people with disabilities sometimes brings one into contact with strangers who ask for one's help. A friend of mine asked me if I would talk to her friend whose son seemed to be giving her a great deal of trouble. I met the woman, who told me that she had fostered her boy when he was a baby and now wanted to adopt him. He was just turning 13 years old and the doctors wanted to put him on medication because his behaviour was so bizarre. She did not want this to happen because she saw him as a darling child whose difficulties might be overcome through education and love. As she spoke, the boy came up the stairs and walked down the passage into the sitting-room.

I did not see the child. What I saw was a shaven-headed figure, wearing a long flowing, silken, blood-red gown. Golden chains, intricately crafted, hung round his neck. His skin was an oiled brown colour, glistening with warm sweat, and his hands moved salaciously over his chest, which bore small breasts. I knew he was a eunuch, neither man nor woman, that he was a shaman with great spiritual powers, and that he cultivated his might and magic by worshipping in a cult that achieved its initiation by the sexual abuse of children. He seemed to be of Indian blood.

And then I saw the boy, charming, fair-haired, with rounded facial features and deep blue eyes. He came up to me, politely shook my hand and bent over to give me a kiss, speaking in a lisping language, just like a girl. The vision had so startled me that I wondered if my jaw had dropped. I pulled myself together, not wanting to say anything to the loving foster mother about what I had seen.

After chatting to the boy, whose charm and warmth were palpable, his mother sent him to do his homework and asked for my advice. I suggested she should concentrate on reinforcing his masculinity. She might get him horse-riding lessons, and perhaps try to enrol him in a school I could recommend, belonging to our organization. I could only sincerely agree with her that medication was not really the answer.

I decided it would be best not to tell her that I had seen his previous life's mission. I had never had such a vision before, but I did not doubt its veracity because it had been so clear and overwhelming. But I was very shaken and wondered how he would live this present life. When I got home, the *National Geographic* magazine had just arrived in the post. Its front cover bore a photograph of a shaman like the one I had seen. The article inside described the Indian sect as being still in existence and the steps that the Indian government was taking to stamp out its terrible practices, the worst being the castrating of small boys, and the prostitution of the girls once they became too old for the cultic sexual rites.

Many years later, I met the same boy as a man. His mother had followed my advice, and he was now living in an adult community, a fully integrated and adjusted person, considering his disability. His charm and warmth and sheer goodness was impressive. He had become a wonderful pianist, and sculptured in clay the most exotic figures, worthy to be called great art. He showed me the very first of these figurines. It was of a person who had breasts and a penis, and stood on a clay ground with its hands outstretched in the graceful gestures of Indian temple dancers. A chain carved over the breasts was as intricately crafted as the gold one in my vision.

Certainly, his disability had settled into what we call Asperger's syndrome, but his desire to reach out to others was unquestioningly strong. All those who lived with him loved him, because his consideration for others was so marked. He wanted to love everyone he met, and suffered from his inability to make real contact. My experience of him was of meeting a human being of real goodness. Moreover, he seemed to have no interest in sexuality at all. What had been so disturbing when I met him as a pre-teen had entirely dissipated, sublimated by his original artistic expression.

I felt an enormous respect and warmth towards this man. Though I had seen who he had once been, I was amazed to feel that I had no judgement over him, only a great admiration. Knowing someone's past life brings a huge experience of freedom. One is face to face with the fact that people make of themselves what their destiny allows, what they have chosen to become.

A Past Life Overshadowing the Present

I had a similar experience a second time, many years later. Strangely, I hardly ever thought about that boy and his past. It was just that, his past, and I left it behind me, until I met him again. But the other seeing of someone's previous life was far more disturbing and made demands upon me. I lived for a very short time with a little girl, very disturbed and violent. She had been taken into care when she was three years old because her mother died and the father abandoned her. She had subsequently been sexually abused by one of the care-workers. She could hit out and attack at any moment, out of the blue, and whilst doing so would cry: 'I didn't mean to, I don't want to, I'm sorry, I'm sorry!' all the while beating one black and blue. The feeling of being beaten by this little mite was as if it came from her own distress, rather than as a dislike of the carer.

Outside these moments she was a darling, clever and bright as a button. Because I loved her dearly, I prayed to her angel every night, and then, one night between waking and sleeping, I saw her, tiny, a mere toddler, and I saw what they did to her in one of Hitler's concentration camps. They performed medical experiments on her brain without using anaesthetic. I will not describe this as it was too horrible.

I knew that her torment was her broken spirit, unable to deal with her past. I could barely live with this knowledge, and found I needed to speak to someone about it. I spoke to a doctor, a close friend of mine. She suggested we form a circle of people who loved her, to pray for her every day. This did not happen, owing to the fact that I seemed to be unable to give a good enough reason for such a circle because I could not talk about what I had seen. Something held me back from explaining the real reason. Apparently I was not allowed to tell anyone other than the doctor. So I prayed for her myself, using a lovely Celtic poem that called upon the guardian angel.

The little girl, after one such attack just before bedtime, said on sobbing breaths as I comforted her with hugs: 'My Mummy always said a prayer with me at bedtime. It goes like this.' And she recited the same prayer I was using for her in the privacy and silence of my room at night.

I do not know what has become of her. Our lives diverged. But for the short time we were together the bruises she inflicted upon me no longer hurt me. And the less I minded about them the less she was compelled to hit out – until the time came when her fists would stop short, just before making contact, and she would say: 'I didn't have to do it this time!'

Understanding the Meaning of Reincarnation

In the years that followed these new other-world experiences, bits of them returned to me – especially at moments when I could not understand or accept another person's behaviour. I suddenly found myself in their shoes, as it were (though never again so vividly as seeing their past lives), which was some-times helpful in dealing with situations. But at other times it was not helpful, because without a real insight into their past it made me susceptible to their feelings and did not always add objectivity.

It seems to me that to have insight into other people's souls requires a huge amount of honesty, otherwise one can find oneself taking sides on issues when compassionate impartiality is what is needed. And to acquire real knowledge is a lifetime's task. Perhaps this was the biggest lesson of that 'dream' con-cerning the Juggler and the Whore, that self-knowledge *must* be worked at, if one is to fulfil one's karma. And where better to learn this than living with people whose lives are directed by their handicap? They cannot step out of their disability on a whim. They are stuck with it for life.

Now I began to understand why we live our lives over and over again. Each life offers another experience, another outlook on the road towards perfection. Perfect truth, perfect health, perfect love can only be learned slowly and painfully by resisting the Juggler's alcoholic suppression of consciousness, and the Whore's enticement to passion without love. A disability may be chosen in order to provide one with particular and strong experiences of the wonder of human love. I still could not answer my son's passionate question, but I could try to help him come to terms with his own skills and perhaps help him to see a way to use them well in his own life.

I learnt for myself that meditation is essential. Without it, one can hardly come to terms with one's own incarnation and karma. So I began to work in earnest. But I did not stop praying, because it comforted me. The more of these 'other side' experiences I was having, the more I needed security in this world as well as in the other.

Talking with the Dead

Then I became very ill and required major surgery. I was very afraid, not being too brave about pain. I had begun to work on a passage in the Bible that meant a great deal to me. At the beginning of the St John's Gospel, the first five verses are lovely to think about – I recited them daily on waking and on going to sleep.

> In the beginning was the Word, and the Word was with God and the Word was God. The same was in the beginning with God. All things were made by him, and without him was not anything made that was made. In him was life, and the life was the light of

men. And the light shineth in darkness; and the darkness comprehended it not.

I recited the familiar words of the Gospel to calm myself before the anaesthetic. Perhaps it is not difficult to imagine that giving up consciousness voluntarily was an uncertain business for me because I never knew if I might not once again cross to the other side. And I did not feel confident about my ability to handle the outcome once more. Maybe I should have had more faith, since I had been able to work with the results so far, but it was a challenge and I did not seek it.

I recovered from the operation very slowly. Everyone around me was hugely supportive, my husband, my children now in their teens, and the community. Although physically I recovered very quickly, it took me two years to arrive in this world again. I could not sleep properly, because I wasn't really properly awake. Words would flow into me from the other side, I talked with friends who had died, heard their words as feeling or colour, or meaning, and then had to try to translate them into real language. Their instructions often came backwards, and when I wrote them down I had to reverse the order to make sense of what they were telling me. Usually I knew who was speaking to me, but sometimes it was a stranger or what seemed to be an angel. I think the 'angels' were actually souls so far on their road to clarity of purpose, and therefore a new incarnation, that their communications came with greater light.

I wrote what they said into poems, as the only real way to express their language. At first it was like following instructions and much of it, when I read what I had written, seemed like rubbish. But I kept the rubbish as a 'learning curve' and began to work at finding the right words to describe accurately the sound, meaning and intentions that came to me. The poems, I decided at that time, were personal, not for public viewing, and I used them to learn about the other side. Now, when I read the first poems, I find they are not rubbish at all. They describe aspects of this world and the other, and how they belong together, this world being a mirror of the other side. They are interdependent worlds, this one in which free choice rules, and mistakes, evil and untruths occur, the other being the *real* world where the ever-living truth creates life.

I learned how language came into being and that it is in danger of losing its life. The way we speak today is dead matter compared to its creative living force in the beginning, when speech first entered the human being. It was formed out of the living breath of the world, each word being a sound picture, a musical meaning of the thing, action or aspect that wanted to be named. Words grew from the essential meaning of everything that came into being in this world. And the sounds that were consequently used to depict the essence depended on the human being's relationship to that essence. Therefore we have so many languages in the world. On the other side, there is only one essence for each thing and it is universally recognized and recognizable. So we don't need to speak on the other side. We *know* into each other and into each thing.

From *The Chymical Wedding of Christian Rosenkreutz* I learned that one of the steps towards initiation can only be rendered through poetry. The experiences cannot be described in prose because it is inclined to be dry, whereas the images are so magnificently coloured and sung. Word pictures that poetry can give are the nearest translation to the life and light and tone of the other side.

The first of these messages came through like the fragment of a play, and I woke up with it after a sleep that was neither absence of consciousness nor a waking dream. My peculiar sleeping habit seemed to topple me from one consciousness into another, and I could move between the two quite easily. In the state of awareness that looked like sleep to the 'normal' waking eye, I moved with other beings in another time-frame, which here, in open daylight, could last a fraction of a second but in the reality of that other place and time could last for hours. I was experiencing time as space, and space as time.

I got out of bed and wrote down the following, as if by dictation. This was the only 'poem' I did not have to reverse, line by line. The voice that spoke it to me still hung in my ear in ringing male tones, formidably authoritative.

The Archangel: O human being, know thyself!

The Masses: We are the bearers of suffering
                   We endure the pain inflicted upon us
                   We carry the burden of life uncomplaining
                   We dig in the dark of the weight of the earth
                   We experience that misery is not of our making
                   We work for the purpose of rest in old age
                   We reflect on the moments of joy that are passed
                   We despise the wealth of our neighbours in
                       righteousness
                   We live simply routinely unexceptionally correctly
                   We recognize Death as freedom from Life.

The Archangel: O human being, know thyself!

The Crowds: We are the seekers of light in the heights
                   We are the bringers of happiness
                   We are the dancers in praise of the Gods
                   We rejoice in our riches our laughter our fun
                   We create our own prayer in fervour and glory
                   We gather together for group meditation
                   We ingest whatever can teach us to fly
                   We adore the creative the new the obscure
                   We worship peace on earth, all men shall have it
                   We disregard Death, turn from darkness to Light.

The Archangel: O human being, know thyself!

The Individual: I bear my body as a vehicle for deeds
I am the ploughman, the sower, the tiller, the reaper
I suffer the pain my own life creates
I know that joy is a transient permanence
I understand that the misery I bear is the road to love
I offer my sorrow as balm to the suffering
I work for the sake of the other's existence
I seek for the light in the eyes of another
I bow to the prayers that arise in my heart
I sing to the music that surrounds my creation
I know that unalterable Death is the doorway from Life
To Life.
    I yearn for the Truth
    In Freedom I tread the path
    In Christ I will find my purpose

The Archangel: O human being, know thyself!

The words, meaning and sounds came without any punctuation as we use it. The meaning was formed because of pauses in the music of the voice, whose words were tones and meaning and form. To make human sense one needs grammar, so in appropriate places I used punctuation, and some words I had to write with capitals because of their absolute meaning.

Quite soon after this one, the creation of language arrived. I did not so much hear this as 'see' it in its creation. But each formation made a word and so I wrote down what it said to me. The sound was like a wild, loud wind, or the pelting of rain on a hollow roof, or the dashing of waves on the rocks. Nevertheless, these nature sounds had meaning, deliberate and crystal clear. This poem came backwards, even the sequence of words in one line needing reversing to make clear sense to anyone reading it, but it has lost some of its majesty in the translation.

The Word

In the beginning was the word
  Murmured by the timelessly rushing river
Reverberated through the rocks of the high ranges
  Babbled in the broken pebbled mountain brook
Breathed in the fluttering filtering leaves
  Torn up grown up raised in the bark of trees
Echoed in the whispering wind
  And the Word was with God.

And the world knew him not
  Computing the concept silicon captured and marked
Caverns of consonants shaped to the tailored perception
  Quick fit exhausted
Drawing the spiralling light of the meaning
  Down to the small analysing of noise
Cut loose from the soul adrift in a mine-shaft
  And the world knew him not.

Mind-caught held transmuted tones
  Clearly capably changed rearranged
Dream-dramas, picture-poets, outpouring voices
  Meaning incumbent, thinking in feeling
Living light between sound and sound
  Sending the air in arcs across chasms of space
Building bridges, moving, propelling articulant speech
  And the word became Flesh.
     I am the Way
       The Truth
       And the Life

I found that I had little choice in the visual form these poems had
to make on paper. And I could not choose their punctuation. Not
only did I have to find the meaning of the thoughts that flowed
into me, but I had to find the exact sounds, so that the words I

used held meaning and sounded right, too. I sweated over them, each one as they came, and could not rest till they looked right, sounded right, had the right meaning and the exact punctuation. And then I had to write them backwards first and reverse them so that they would hold meaning for people here who were not on the other side!

Clearly, from the content of these two poems, my pre-occupation with the first words of St John's Gospel were finding an answer from the other side. And my need to understand why human beings reincarnate was also becoming clearer. The role of the Juggler and the Whore started to make sense too. The masses in the first poem belong to the Juggler and the crowds to the Whore. If they were — as images of the whole human being — to become united, humanity would lose heart for life and sink down into matter, become as stones of the earth, or fly away into spiritualism and become crazed inhuman madmen. We have to follow the individual path of acceptance of destiny, of realization that I make my life by the way I live it. I can be free only if I take responsibility for what I think, feel and do, because everything I think, feel and do affects the people and the world around me directly and therefore the whole world and all of humanity indirectly. That I and the world are one is quite clear from what the Archangel said, and that what I do, feel and think creates my destiny and the destiny of others.

I began to look forward to these conversations with beings on the other side and to relish the answers I found, though some of the poems took me years to understand and some of them I still don't quite get. As for instance this one:

Becoming Human

Slow Tone
Beating the hot red drum
Pulsating, pounding the dark warmth

Mounting, moulding, making the dark warmth
Intoning the form of the long future
Founding the molten lead
Red in the heat of the mould
Still, slow moving Tone.

Slight, shining Melody
Lilting larklike in golden trill
Lifting Light slipping brightly
Trembling lightly into warmth
Raising Life into warmth
Bringing Light, linking sound
Running from low to high
Moving from drum-past to living Melody.

Coloured Harmony
Binding the down-bent warmth
Singing the lilting living Melody
Into related sound
Moving silver summoning mood
Ebbing silent slow waters
Reflecting, raying the rainbow
Creating myriad Harmony.

Tone beat, living Melody, myriad Harmony
Sounding in steady quickening speed
Forming foundation to matter
Shining in lilting Light
Comforting marvel of Harmony
Speeding, separating, demarcating
Into the rhythm of breath
Uniting all sound.

Wholeness parted
Clarity, sharpness, Space
Brought to meaning through rhythm in Time
Spoken out of the dark warmth of Tone

Sung out of the Light of Melody
Given feeling through the marvel Harmony
Speech freed on the breath of Man
Tone, Melody, Harmony become I AM.

Is this how we are formed as an archetype of humanity? Or is this about the sexual creation of a baby? I think maybe it is about both. Spiritually, before we are born, we go through the poem's process in order to prepare for incarnation. And when our parents meet in the sexual act here in this world, it echoes the power of creation in the passion, warmth, melody and harmony of human love. Therefore, to make a baby carelessly or without intention is so deep an evil; and so much misery follows the birth and life of an unwanted child. The Juggler and the Whore have won that fight. But, thankfully, there are more wanted than unwanted human beings in the world.

Words from the other side just seemed to pour out into me. And those words that required capitals did so because they weren't simply words. They were descriptions of beings, angelic creatures whose existence depended on recognizing their reality by speaking their names. I had to write as I heard and saw. And then I could take the time to think about and understand what I had been told.

Between these marvellous communications were times of deep distress. I did not want to live in this world at all. The other was so tempting. But I also loved my life here, with my children, my husband, my friends and my work with disabled people. I wanted to have everything at once, and this is not a good state of mind! One must choose, between this world and that, as long as one has a physical body. Or one must learn to direct and control those other experiences, legitimizing them, so to speak, or else they will drive you crazy.

Clearly, if we live between the two worlds there are temptations. We cannot reach into the other world just like that. We are thrown, as I was, or we have to find a way through our religious or meditative discipline. This is hard to do because of the temptations organized by the Evil. However, there are beings who guard the way to the other side, who show themselves as grotesque deformed animal creatures – two or three such beings guard the space between. Behind them is darkness and behind that is living light. I saw these things and translated them into the poems. The poems quoted above were only the first ones. Others came thick and fast and each one gave me a little more knowledge. They came over a period of ten years. And then they stopped.

I stopped them myself. I took advice from a friend, because they were beginning to consume my consciousness. I felt the messages were overwhelming me. I would wake up with a poem demanding 'birth' and would have to labour until it had acquired its rightful shape and meaning. If this happened whilst I was meant to be working, I would have to stop doing things and sit down to write! I felt dictated to, out of control of my life here on this side of existence. To regain control, I began to work at writing my own poetry. What a successful way to kill inspiration. I am really and truly no poet!

Dark Guardians

In these states of 'neither here nor there' consciousness, I met three beasts. You come across these creatures when you arrive at the point where the worlds meet. They are there to warn us, to make us want to be clear and clean before reaching the world of light. They hover over a crack in the earth's crust from which darkness rises. You can get a glimpse of this if you concentrate on becoming aware of the moment you are about to fall asleep, and make yourself wake up. It is like jumping over an abyss. But if you stop, mid-jump, then the darkness rises and the beasts come out. Behind them, over the darkness, is the light that calls with pure goodness.

They are fearful creatures because they live inside us, as well as exist in their own right. One is greyish blue with skin like an elephant, rough and folded. He has a caricature of a human face, no eyes but two dark streaming raying sockets and bat's wings. He saps energy, life, light and hope. Another is orange turning to mud, face and fur like a cat, ruffled and prickly. He makes one turn boneless, drains the ability to act. The other one I saw was so far in the distance, so deep in the abyss, that all I could make out was a greyish yellow, like pus-filled flesh and a blunt dog's snout. I could not say what he does because I only glimpsed him, but the sensation he caused in me I cannot describe. I buried it somewhere inside me.

Mostly, I did nothing to reach the terrible place of change. I just got there. Sometimes I could not leave it again without praying to my angel who never failed me, embracing me in golden warmth. But in general, the extraordinary communications of light from the other side centred me and the terrible place was a passing moment of hesitation.

The Double and the Nine Ranks of Spirit Beings

The oddest thing about these experiences was the way they forced me to live my daily life. I could not at first behave 'normally'. I would either find myself diving into everything as though meeting it for the first time, or would discover myself to be so far outside everything that I saw it all from a vast distance. It was rather frightening. It made me react to any stimulation with emotion. But as time passed, I seemed to get used to this extreme way of living. I dealt with it, as I already described, by staying in bed as much as I could. I felt safe there, as though anchored in a kind of reality that stabilized me. It gave me time to digest this seesaw life experience. Going inside things made me aware of the fearful dark depths that material bodies give our powers of thinking and feeling and actions. The darkness there is grim. I became very frightened until the following insight was opened to me.

The Double

In the valley of the shadow of death
Walks the Un-man
Barbarous twisted statue
Creeping upright, appearance a deception
A distortion of humanity
Shaded creature, companion nightmare
Imperturbably causing the darkness
Making the action impenetrable
Masking creation from the created
Mortifying, petrifying movement
Trailing un-truth banner-like
In windless airless space.

This I, my Other Self
Swells to bloated carnality
Leering and lying
Curling and primping
And I must bear this Otherness
Always in the valley of my soul.

Once this had been written down and was, as it were, outside me so that I could think about it, the fear left me. It is true of every human being that the dark side is as present as the light side, true too of nature and everything in the world. I found it easier to live with this truth, once I could look it in the face.

Now I could get up and be part of life again in an ordinary

everyday sense. And then the surging tidal force within me took me to a place outside of me. It always took me unawares, in the middle of perfectly ordinary activities, like shopping or cooking. I would find myself high up somewhere, looking down on or through the physicality of things and see 'inside' them. The nearest comparison I can make is as though I were outside the earth's orbit, on another star and gazing at the earth as a globe, and at the same time seeing every little detail of people, events, nature and the earth's core. Very dizzying!

Unfortunately, I quite liked this feeling, and felt drawn to creating it. However, I knew it was dangerous, and if I wasn't quite mad I would get there if I played with it! So I tried to be conscious as a centred being whenever it happened. This meant that no matter where I was or what time of day or night I made myself write down what I heard and saw.

On one such occasion, I happened to be walking across the farmyard. Above me, the lime tree towered in the spring sunlight, its blood-red buds about to burst on Easter day. The angels swirled around it, moving and creating its very existence from a substance that reverberated in differing speeds of sound, each tone becoming another twig, branch or layer of bark. I could see the rising tide of sap within the transparent browns of the bark. The living strength of it hardened into a dark cross within the trunk, which now sprouted the branches and buds of the tree. And from those buds dripped living blood, falling down into the earth, right to its core, from whence sprang all life.

And then I was standing looking at the lime tree, beautiful in the spring sunlight, a few sparrows twittering on the telegraph pole beside it. I felt as if I had been standing on that spot for aeons of time, but in truth it had been only a second, here on this side of things. I walked into the nearest house, stole their shopping list, because no one was there to ask and it was the only bit of paper I could lay my hands on at that moment, and wrote down what I had seen and heard!

Poems that arrived in this dynamic way were different, easier to write, because they flowed, whereas the poems from the depths had to be dug up or carved out. The language I used had, needless to say, to come from human speech. So the images unfortunately became fixed and identified, whereas in reality they were in constant motion, transformative sounds. I knew I was really seeing the spirit of nature, the creative word that is frozen into matter.

Easter

I saw the angels holding the sun's bright light
And the archangels challenging the wavering dark
And the archai rising with the sun.

The exusiai are swelling in the warmth of the wind
Kyriotetes are quickening the clear bird-song
And the dynamis are bringing all to birth.

I saw the cherubim weaving in the tracery of twigs
And the seraphim singing in the light green leaves
And the thrones' power thrusting in the trunk.

The cross is cut from the trunk and limbs
And life and light run down with the sap
And the blood drip-drops, drip-drops.

On the earth, in the earth, through the earth and deep
Flows the light and life in which I breathe
Till the roses riot in the sun.

The names of the nine angelic beings were the only names I knew at the time. So I used them. One could just as well have used the variety of names we humans have given to the spirits in other religious traditions.

Getting Back to Work

The light on the other side called me. I did not know how to reach that light in my own right and so fell into the inner darkness. I took such a long time to recover my health because the disorientating effect of being within things and then entirely outside them, whilst still maintaining the power to observe what was happening, exhausted me. But eventually I woke up to the fact that I was here, in this world, and I would not get anywhere by remaining between. I would have to get up and live here properly. So I got up and, as the years passed, gained my strength. Contact with the other side and its creatures faded.

All the time, my friends and family stood by me and did not think I was mad or having a breakdown. They trusted me and I felt very privileged and grateful. Their belief in me allowed me to explore responsibly the experiences, and to translate them into something useful for daily life. And when I stepped back into care-work again, they welcomed me back. Community, if practised with honesty, is very creative and caring. People really look after each other.

So I took on a household, together with my husband, with teenagers with disabilities and enjoyed the challenges enormously. Everyday life seemed so precious, every detail fun, even the bad bits that naturally happen when living with adolescents. The smelly feet, the moods, the love affairs, the arguments were all a part of my daily life and my own children were as much a part of the teenage scene as were the residents. The age gap between the residents and my children and the volunteers was closing rapidly and I felt like everybody's unwanted mother. Unwanted, that is, until they were in some kind of trouble and then I was supposed to wave some magic wand and, like Wonderwoman, bale them out. However, we also had so much fun together. I enjoyed being a part of their explorations into life, experience and the wide, wide world.

Those were great years and I felt better and better. I still went through days of diminished strength, both physically and mentally, but the weird sensation of walking next to myself and observing myself as if I were a stranger was hardly a problem any more. And my body gained health again.

Tuning in to the World's Pain

I was 43 years old when next I crossed over. I had got used to the fact that in some vague and indeterminate way the other side was always present, but I did not go there in full awareness and I was not called either, except through the poems that were still working through me at that time. But something new and uncomfortable became a continuous companion.

I would wake up in the middle of the night, or almost lose consciousness in the middle of my working day, because of physically nauseating feelings that attacked my midriff. They hurt, coming in waves, and though I felt them physically I knew they were upsets of my soul and not really of my stomach. These horrible waves preceded a disaster. Sometimes I knew what the disaster would be, such as the attack on my son in Johannesburg. He was travelling in South Africa and did not take the advice given to avoid certain areas. So he walked straight into a mugging, and had some of his belongings taken. Because he ran he was not knifed or otherwise injured, but it was a tricky moment in his life.

I felt so ill the day it happened I could hardly function, snapping at those around me in a most unreasonable manner. When the phone rang I knew it was him, because the churning warning sensation instantly ceased.

However, mostly I did not know until some dreadful event

happened. The minute I knew consciously of the disaster, the waves ceased. Sometimes I heard about several terrible happenings, but only one of them would stop the nausea. I felt as if I was being tuned in to certain destinies, but not to others. There was no pattern to them, and I have still not been able to find one. The sensations would build up and then inexplicably stop. I would then hear, read or be told about an earthquake, a bomb exploding, a car pile-up or someone's illness.

I began to time these attacks, looking at the clock and the date of their commencement, and their ending, and comparing them to the information of the events that reached me in the ordinary way. In this way, I hoped to discover why I was being forewarned of things to which I could not find any personal connection. I am still working on it. It is, however, very clear to me that the warnings are real and directed each time to one particular event. That I cannot always make the connection is my fault and does not negate the validity of the communication. I can more reliably connect when the events occur to close friends or family. Apparently one needs to be very in tune with other human beings to lock in to their karma. Or perhaps it is necessary to practise the awareness, but I have not yet found a reliable, meditative way in which to do this. Addressing a person's angel can make the path between smoother and more easily accessible, but how to work with the angels of people whom one does not know is not yet clear to me.

Helping the Dead

Meanwhile, my daily life still involved people with special needs. They are wonderful people, real, honest, challenging, funny, tiresome and hard work, and they make such very good friends. Just as with any human being, you get on better with some than with others. One boy was a very special friend of mine.

Black-haired and black-tempered, with a great sense of humour, he could be extremely trying to people who did not know him. But we got on very well. Sometimes familiarity isn't helpful to a young person's development. The young man was reaching 20 years and I could see that my knowing him so very well might become a stumbling block. One can become stuck in old habits of relationship. So we decided that he should live in another house and get to know other people, to broaden his horizons and to prepare him for adult life.

He moved and was very unhappy at first, finding it hard to adapt to other ways. But as the year progressed he found his feet, more or less. He visited often, which was lovely for both of us. Then he went on an outdoor pursuits week and we heard he had got lost on the mountain. The nausea, which filled me as soon as they had left our premises, instantly vanished. But my whole being centred on him, as though I was transported inside him. I could feel a great fear, and was overwhelmed by anxiety that was not my own.

They set up a search. I followed it all by means of the telephone. At regular intervals it rang with more news of no news. I lived in a continuous hubbub of other people's fears, speculations, plans, reports. The internal panic that had filled my being also continued, though I was aware that it was not my terror, but his. There was absolutely no peace and time to think about him constructively. The world was far too noisy.

I tried to find a quiet moment for him, using my meditation time to be with him. By midnight I knew he had died. They said there was still hope, but I could *feel* that he had gone over to the other side. There was a sense of purpose and finality within me and around me, which I understood to be coming from my friend. My husband tried to calm me down because I thought that it was my fault for trying to move him too fast into adulthood.

The next day they found him, drowned in shallow water, naked, his clothes folded neatly on the shoreline. The follow-up investigation was as noisy and official as these things always are, and concluded that his death had been an accident. I found that I could not say to people that he had chosen his moment to cross over. It would sound as though I were insisting that his death was suicide. Perhaps in our terms, here on this side, we might call it suicide, but in my friend's soul he had merely completed his time here and was ready to go over. I wondered if this had been his burden, the knowledge that he would only be here for a short lifetime. Was this why he suffered deep depressions, showing his pain by attacking others?

The night he died, I crossed over, just before falling asleep. I stood on the shore beside a black river, deep and slow, moving like the waters in a still lake. On the other shore the light shone, bright and radiant, as bright as the sun, but I could look at it with my naked eye and it neither burned, nor blinded me. Squatting at the river's edge, his back to the light, was my friend, arms outstretched towards me, his mouth open, calling. I saw him as a silhouette before the brightness of the light, and at the same time could see him in full colour, blue eyes, black hair, white skin, because he was naked. He was in a place of living greenness, a lawn that doesn't exist on this side of the river, glowing with warmth and promise. But he could not see the life on which he squatted, nor the light behind him that called lovingly and patiently for his attention. The light was one bright luminosity.

I wanted to answer his call, but he could not hear me, and I could not hear the meaning of his plea. I saw that he could not see the light behind him, did not even know that it was there. He saw only the darkness of the world he had left, saw it as a blank into which he could no longer wake up.

And I could not go to him, nor make him hear me. He seemed to want me to take his hands, to hold him and reassure him, but I could not cross that river. I wasn't allowed to do so. I knew I should be able to get him to listen to me, but his fear deafened him to my voice, as he was blind to the light. I saw that he was trapped in his fear, as one is imprisoned in a windowless cell with soundproofed walls.

I woke my poor husband, describing what I was seeing, feeling desperate because I couldn't answer the poor boy's begging. We talked a bit and I tried to go to sleep but every time I shut my eyes, there I was again, seeing the pleading crouched figure, unable to reach him. This went on night after night for six weeks.

We had gone on holiday to Crete, a wonderful country, light, perfumed and full of interest. Part of me did the tourist bit, but part of me stood at the river, trapped, not knowing how to help my friend. The trapped feeling got stronger and stronger. Slowly it dawned on me that his had been no accidental dying but a free choice. However, this choice trapped him, held him fast in the moment of dying, repeating his crossing over and over, so that he could not move from that moment.

When we came home I went to see my friend, the priest. I knew I was meant to do something to help but I did not know what and needed help myself. I was exhausted from lack of sleep. He told me that I should go to the river (which I did anyway, called by the boy), and that I should show him how to turn round to look at the light. He needed to recognize that it was there to welcome him, that in the light he would find his comfort and a way forward.

I wondered how this would work out. I had never yet been able to go voluntarily to the river. When I tried, it was just a poor memory, not the real thing at all. The real journey only happened at night, between sleeping and waking. However, I had to do something, and his advice had been good when it concerned the little girl.

So that evening, I sat in a chair and went to the river. There were no beasts, and I was instantly there. I spoke to my friend, telling him of the light, seeing its brightness and asking him to turn. He did not move, but cried more quietly. Evening after evening I did this, and slowly I saw that he was moving round, bit by bit, still squatting in fear, still blind to the light, still only seeing the empty darkness, but slowly turning.

I slept soundly every night during this process, and my days were easy and clear. It took a week of this earth time until he was squatting, his back to me and his face to the light, his arms now reaching towards the new life. The evening that he opened his eyes and stood up was the last time I saw him. He held his arms out, now in welcome, rather than beseeching, and raised his head. Though still a silhouette, I could see his face, the grimace of weeping now dawning into wonder. The light was moving, changing form into individual purpose. I wanted to see the special light that belonged to my friend, to see it in its own separate form, but I was thrown back to ordinary awareness. I felt as though *wanting* had been a mistake. One cannot *demand* on the other side.

The next evening when I reached the river, the other side was empty, only the light remained. I knew he had gone into the light and that the beings who lived within it, who created its brightness, would help him. I say 'they' because in the course of that week, I saw that the light was differentiated and consisted of multitudes of beings of light, one in their mission yet individually linked to each soul that crosses. Imagine the ocean, vast and surging, a moving wholeness consisting of millions of individual droplets. We see the water as one body, yet each drop is an ocean unto itself. Each of us has our own light waiting for us. I was deeply sorry that I could not see my friend's light meeting him, but I knew it would be a greeting of love and support.

I felt free, free to grieve properly. Grieving is important, especially for those who cross over deliberately, because they are confused to find that consciousness is not done and over with the dying, it only changes. Not having a material body doesn't make you non-existent. It makes you exist in a much more powerful way. Your sight, hearing, knowledge is so much greater without the material limits that bodies give. So he had been frightened. He had been frightened when dying, preparing himself by folding his clothes and offering up his life in this world. And he had expected it to be the end, when it proved to be the beginning. He could not see the new world, because he was focused on the old.

I wondered why the beings of light couldn't help him, why they needed a human being on this side to tell him they were there. Later on I found an answer to this question, but at that time I was left to ponder on it. But I learned that grieving is to carry the memory of a person's life for them, until they are used to their new existence. Grieving is like handing over, if it is carried out with knowledge of the light. If one grieves only for one's own loss of the loved one, one binds them to the river's edge and that makes it harder for them to move on.

For many years I included him in my prayers, wondering where he had gone once he entered the light. That light held such power, and assurance of something more, that I longed to know, but I could only reach the river on this side. And when I tried to go there after he had moved on, I could not.

The other thing that puzzled me was not meeting the beasts or seeing the abyss. That too I only understood years later. There were no more visits to the river for many years. I almost forgot about it, except when I prayed for my friend and then, if I tried to go there, the scene was always empty. So I began to think it might have been all in my imagination.

The Power of Prayer

Meanwhile, life moved on and brought new people, new challenges and I grew older. My relationship towards prayer was a growing one and I began to notice that if I prayed for the good to come about, even if that good might be something different from that for which I prayed, situations and people who got stuck could be moved into more positive arenas. I found then, and still do today, that prayer is intensely practical. But not always in the way that one expects. What I deem to be the right course may not be right for someone else. So I learned to pray for the good by itself, rather than with conditions attached to it.

My life continued in its humdrum fashion until it was turned upside down by the advent of a 14-year-old street-wise boy. He arrived on our doorstep accompanied by a social worker who was resigned to hear that we too, like the hundreds of other places they had visited, would refuse to take in the boy. He was exceedingly charming, smart, dyslexic, manipulative and highly disturbed. He came from a background the like of which one reads about in novels, only fact is so often worse than fiction. The more we got to know the boy, and the closer we grew to him, the more remarkable he seemed to us – because he knew how to love. He had been used abominably in his short life and yet could open up his heart and soul to people who extended the hand of friendship.

However, given his background, he could do nothing but run away from himself. He stayed nowhere for very long, always returning to his friends in the street. They made no demands upon him because they shared his dreadful life experience, whereas social workers were to be feared and distrusted, as were care-workers and the like. But he loved our house, appreciated the warm baths and good food, liked to be clean, and loved art. He wanted to stay with us but could not help messing things up all the time. He had to test and test and test. When things became too difficult, he would find ways to express his apologies, which we learned were warnings before absconding. Then he ran again, climbing out of the upstairs window and down the drainpipe. He had no fear of death. The police brought him back every time he ran, a review would follow, social workers and men from the Department would visit, new resolutions were taken together with him, and for a time he stayed put. Then he ran again and everything went full circle.

One day he had enough. He left and refused to come back. He said he was not fit to be with us, loved us, but could not stay. His home was on the streets where he belonged. This time, everyone agreed that he would have to learn by his mistakes. He had shown that no matter how much alcohol he consumed, he was not an alcoholic. No matter how many drugs he took, he did not get hooked. He remained, despite his corrupt experiences, an innocent. Therefore, they reasoned, he would come to no harm. We would have to let him go. Besides, obviously what we had to offer did not meet his needs.

So we did not fetch him back and I could not sleep at night. The lifestyle we had given him would have spoilt him for permanent street-living. I knew some harm would befall him. He was so good looking, so innocent, and so trusting, it was bound to happen that older, more corrupt people would take advantage of him. Though clearly he had been abused, he seemed to know nothing about sex or pain, and met life head on with trust and honesty. But sometimes he would say quietly: 'You have no idea how lonely and cold it can be by the river.'

He had been gone a week when I woke, breathless and panicked, in the middle of the night. I could not rest. I knew something had happened to him. A voice had woken me up, not with words, but with intent.

The next morning, as soon as was decent, I rang his social

worker. She said that he was in hospital, in intensive care, almost dead from an overdose. She phoned again, the next day to tell me that he had not taken the drug himself. He had fooled about with someone else's woman, and that person had cornered him and forced the drug down his throat. A passer by had kindly and anonymously informed the police, which was how he came to be rescued. He was happy enough in hospital but could not stay there indefinitely.

I went away to talk to his angel. I asked that the right future would be opened up for him. I pledged myself to do everything I could to get him to a school that I knew could help him. This would involve a great deal of manoeuvring and I realized, as I made my promise, that I might not succeed. But his angel could open the doors, if it lay in his rightful destiny.

With this resolve and confidence in his angel, I began to telephone, first the school. They answered that they would have a vacancy in three months' time, and agreed at least to consider him and offer an interview. Next I spoke to his social worker, who, to my great surprise, not only knew the school but had had the same idea herself. The senior social worker, when I contacted him, also knew the school, had visited it some years ago and thought it eminently suitable. By this time, I was not surprised any more. We agreed to tackle the Department together, three being more powerful than one. So far so good.

My biggest hurdle, however, was our own organization. We had decided that we did not meet his needs. Now I went to them and said that if we did not take him back, at least temporarily until the new school could admit him, he might die. They said it was not our concern. He had caused enough disruption. We could no longer help him. I asked them to allow me to commit myself to him for the three months. I would take him on completely, guaranteeing no problem, until he could be moved on. To my amazement, they agreed.

The Department was a pushover. The boy's story had hit the newspapers and they were challenged to solve his case or be called negligent. He was still legally a minor and therefore their responsibility, since the mother had declared herself unfit to care for him. My offer to keep him until the new school could take him seemed like a godsend to them. The fact that this school was overseas and would cost them an arm and a leg did not phase them.

Then we had to talk to the boy. I met him, in the social-work department, and asked him if the arrangements I was making met with his approval. Of course, he wanted to visit the school and see it before making up his mind. (He insisted upon this with a huge grin, well aware that nothing could be done without his agreement and enjoying the attention and anxiety we all felt on his behalf!) Also, his mother had to give her consent.

Now I had reached the hardest part in my negotiations with his angel. I had to approach her angel too! I decided to talk to his mother personally, hoping that this would be the most honest and least difficult way forward. In the course of our painful negotiations she accused me of taking him away from her. This was quite true from her perspective. When I agreed with her, she instantly changed her tune, agreeing to visit the school with him. (More money from the Department and a free three-day holiday for them both!)

They visited and loved the place. His mother consented to his attending school across the water, provided he would come back for the holidays. And so he returned to me, temporarily. He promised that he would not run away, and kept that vow. Perhaps it had something to do with the fact that in the time I had known him he had grown taller and lost some of his boyish prettiness. His 'mates' on the street no longer wanted to protect him as they had when he was still a boy. Now he posed a male threat and they did not look after him any more. However that may be, he agreed to cooperate with us. In return, I had promised that he would cause no trouble, so he went everywhere with me for three months, causing *me* a great deal of trouble by being good with me and horrible with everyone else on the rare occasions that I could not take him along. Then he moved to the new school.

I felt, throughout this time, that someone else was opening the doors, was arranging everyone to be exactly where they should be, in order to make the boy's path smooth. And this was how his life ran, for two and a half years. Everything was not always so easy for his new teachers and carers, but he hung on to his school and made progress in most things. I relished the letters he wrote to me, and visited him every holiday in the children's home. He turned 18 and went into a black depression. His houseparents, with whom he had formed an astonishing and warm relationship based on mutual trust, realized that his time was up. He had been offered training, but refused, saying his real life was on the streets. He thanked them for their kindness, expressed his love for them, but insisted that now he had to go back where he belonged.

Praying for him only told me that his choice was his own. I was not given to see what destiny waited for him. If I were true to my promise, I would have to let go in trust that what we had done for him would leave its mark and help him wherever he would now go. He is always on my mind and in my prayers, but I know that one cannot make demands on spiritual beings. They know more than we do, here in this life, because they see all the lives that a single soul lives as one whole, whereas we see our 'now' life as being the only one, at best as one in a series of lives. I am certain that he is safe with his angel, though I know that his daily life must be a terrible struggle. I kept my promise not to want anything for him that did not belong to his destiny.

My Own Guardian Angel

The experience of the boy's angel was the second time I really and truly knew and recognized the power of guardian angels – although it was the first time that I consciously and deliberately went out to work with it, as one would go out and choose a library book. Every encounter previous to this had been over-shone by a great deal more of faith than real practical wisdom, except one. That it was possible for me to rely on his angel grew out of the most dynamic encounter I had ever had with my own angel.

I received a letter from a former colleague that informed me that I had been in direct contact with someone who was now accused of alleged criminal actions. He wrote that I might be implicated. The shock was enormous. I searched through my memory, bringing up in very clear details my so-called involve-ment. I saw that though I had not acted in any way against the law I could probably not prove this.

For some days I worried about it, feeling more and more stressed, on behalf of the accused, but – to be honest – even more on my own behalf. The usual sort of scenarios ran through my head: a ruined career, a besmirched name, the effect on my family, and fear of imprisonment. No matter how many times I told myself these things could not happen to me, I knew that they could because I did indeed know the accused and we had worked together for a short time.

One night I reached my nadir. I lay, unsleeping, cold and very afraid. But in that black moment I felt warmth, like the enfolding of the softest mohair blanket, wrapping itself around me. I lay not in my bed of selfish fear but cradled in feather-down wings of glowing warmth. All around me the room was tinged with lapping flames that caressed my cowardly body. The flames burnt through me with a gentle heat that cleansed and healed and I was entirely rested and refreshed. No words came to me but meaning flowed around me telling me that what lay in my destiny was always good, even though it might appear to my limited physical vision as bad. I slept peacefully after this wonderful angelic 'bath', no longer afraid of anything. It was this hugely encouraging experience that gave me the confidence to employ angelic help with the boy's destiny, and showed me how to ask without wanting or making demands.

The Dead Help the Living

Though *we* cannot make demands upon beings who inhabit the spiritual world, *they* can, and do, make demands upon us. We usually experience these communications as commands, rather than as unreasonable requests. Sometimes we don't want to respond, and then our destinies get tangled in events we cannot quite fathom, but we are aware within ourselves of the origins of the confusion. Once we offer these difficult moments to our angel, they can be cleared up — but not always in the way we expect.

I had become involved in teaching young volunteers how to live and work with special needs people. I had been invited to work with the course faculty, a not inconsiderable compliment. Strangely, however, I found it challenging and often frustrating, because the main focus was on teaching and therapy rather than on the actual day-to-day care work, which is the major part of life in a community with people with learning difficulties. No matter how hard I tried to include this aspect in the training course, the other two always took precedence. So I began to wonder if I was in the right job.

I worried about it for some time, talking about it to friends and colleagues, all of whom agreed with me and encouraged me to continue the good fight in defence of care workers. Then a very powerful lady in our organization died. Her contribution to our work had been in the co-founding of villages for adults with special needs, the chief emphasis being on daily life and work. She was a remarkable person in that no matter how busy she was she always had an open door. You could talk to her about anything. On arrival, she would welcome you and offer you a cup of tea. She would sit down and listen, sharing with you her vast store of common sense. So that afterwards you could go away feeling that life's little niggles had fallen into their proper place.

I attended her funeral, and was amazed at how many people came. It ended up like a festival of thanksgiving for a human life well spent. A year passed and I woke up one morning with her firm voice ringing in my ear, as though she were standing over my bed: 'Don't just think about it. Do it!' Her sharp and clear English tones thrust me out of bed and I stood, shivering in the winter morning, both shocked and exhilarated. Very well, I thought, I will! I phoned the first friend who entered my head, and shared my ideas with her. She suggested another friend, who suggested another, and so the circle was completed. We met and formed a course designed to be a path of development for homemakers on how to create therapeutic homes for people with special needs. Our aim was to raise awareness of the value of care in the home as the foundation for the ability to be an adjusted member of society.

Throughout the forming of this new course, I felt entirely in the old lady's hands, simply following her instructions. I did not feel used or guided. I just listened to that voice and did whatever came next. Once the course was up and running, the instructions ceased. I knew we were on our own now, but the sense of satisfied praise has stayed with me down the years. When people comment on how much they appreciate the support and affirmation they can resource from the course, I want to turn round and thank the old lady rather than take the compliment myself. But of course it was because I heard her, and listened to her, that such help could be created for the forgotten servants that care workers often feel themselves to be. So I thank those kind people and do not mention the old lady across on the other side.

It is not always the voice of angels that we hear. It can be the voice of people from the other side, whose interest and love for human deeds keeps them in touch with us. From experiences that I describe further on in this book, I think it is often the dead who reach out to us, those with whom we have had very strong connections, who want to help us carry out our tasks. Just because they are working from the other side does not mean they are ineffectual. It does, however, mean that we have to learn to hear or see them, and here the angels help us. They soften our hard material ears and eyes.

The Power of Angels

Shortly after working with the boy's angel, I came into contact with another young boy whose life had been very similar, only worse. He had been abused, sexually, physically and emotion- ally, from a very young age. Though taken into care, the scars remained and he was the most challenging child I have ever lived with. I found to my horror that I had to make a supreme effort to love him. Every day, I had to say to myself that within his damaged little soul lay a jewel of love. Without this convic- tion, I don't think I could have coped with the behaviour he displayed, casually and without any apparent feeling for other people. He acted out of supreme egotism, other children driving him to extremes of meanness and cruelty.

And then I saw his angel. We had gone to the church service on Sunday. He sat by himself, as he liked to do, fiddling with his trouser belt buckle. I sat at the side from him, two rows back so that I could keep an eye on him and rescue the situation should it be necessary. At one point in the service, we all got up to sing a hymn. Behind him a being arose, huge, beautiful, awe-inspiring. He stood so tall and raised a hand to lay it on the boy's shoulder. The hand was black, shining like the wing of a butterfly, and I could see that the whole body was made of butterfly's wings, differentiations of glowing polished coal-black satin appearing like millions of shimmering, all-seeing eyes over the whole form. The might and power of the being was both an assurance of goodness and a deep dark threat. The angel spread his dark wings over the boy whom I could see through his transparent beauty as the boy stood casually on one foot, the other slightly sideways, singing his heart out. The being's might swelled and filled the room, towering into eternity. I wanted so much to see his face, but I was afraid of what it might say to me. The boy sat down and the angel was gone, but the sheen of polished blackness hung around him. I knew that his life was going to be as hard in the future as it had been in the past and I wanted to weep for his tiny spark of goodness buried so deep inside him. And indeed, a year later, we were obliged to move him on to a more secure home.

The extraordinary thing about this angel was the powerful emanation of might far above morality as we humans know it. The goodness I recognized was not one so puny as to judge between right or wrong. It was rather an assurance of absolute being-hood, of goodness as a being, that moves and shakes the soul of all creation. One could not bargain, cheat or lie in the face of such grandeur. We judge by such small and insignificant paltry standards because we cannot encompass our successive lives as one whole. We can only see in part where our destiny — or another's destiny — is heading.

Because I have seen how grand and powerful his angel is, I have no fear for him, but I must admit that sorrow spreads its pall whenever I think about him. The angels work as they must, bringing destiny to fulfilment. They judge neither good nor bad, but simply carry out their task as guardians of our individual lives on earth. I understood this quite clearly by the posture of his angel, hand protectively on his shoulder, guiding him forward, and by the colour and majesty of his terrible form, black and beautiful and unrelentingly all-knowing. Nevertheless, suffering is the sure and certain consequence.

The Death of My Mother-in-Law

The other side began to surge towards me again when my mother-in-law died. I was past my fiftieth birthday, a great threshold, where my life appeared to have a new beginning, a new thrust in vitality. I was now a grandmother, enjoying life from this new perspective. How extraordinarily different it is to take care of one's children than it is of one's grandchildren! I felt as if only now I really knew how to be a mother.

My mother-in-law had been ill for some time with cancer, and knew she was dying. She had managed to visit us six months earlier for the christening of her great-granddaughter. She was a great personality, quiet, disciplined and humorous. Very much taller than me, I had at first felt intimidated by her. But the more I got to know her, the more her stillness and economy of movement became an outer image for me of her inner discipline. She rarely made judgments, had a strong sense of humour and I almost never heard her complain. I grew to love and admire her, though always with a slight reserve based on the greatest of respect. Her inner self seemed to be looking at me, as though asking me a question that I could not answer.

She had spent most of her adult life on an island in the Caribbean, an island that had no natural drinking water. All water was either shipped in or distilled from the sea. The image of dryness, of no natural water, made me think of the struggle for life that inhabiting such an island would entail. She said that she experienced it to be a place of materialism. To satisfy her inner ideals, all she could find was the Scouts movement. She devoted herself to these ideals, finding in them a source of inner discipline, a commitment to the good, and an expression of love towards humanity. She made these principles into her own personal way of life. It was only after her death that we read her notebooks where she had jotted down these vows.

To be prepared meant, for her, to be open to destiny, to challenges in life, to suffering and joy. It meant to do one's best in the face of adversity, quietly and willingly. It meant to recognize and encourage the best in each person. It meant not to judge others, nor oneself, but to work for the good to become manifest. It meant using life as a force for good. She was a very practical person, skilful in so many things, a great reader in her old age. She still baked her own bread until, in the last six months of her life, her illness prevented it.

Loyalty was second nature to her. Whatever one did or thought, one knew she stood by, never judging, but able to listen. Her quality of listening was like a mirror in which one saw oneself more clearly. She never probed or prodded for confidences, but we all knew we could tell her anything. At first, this aspect of her frightened me. I was used to a more chatty sort of family life. But eventually I grew to appreciate the trust she placed in her fellow human beings, and felt able to talk to her without fear. Only then could I really say that we understood each other, once our barriers of different cultures and habits were overcome.

We flew over to Holland for her funeral and arrived late in the night. She lay, serene, severe and beautiful, in her own bed. Her skin was sallow, and lines of suffering were etched around her closed eyes. She looked rather masculine, surprisingly for a woman whose femininity was unquestioned. She had always had a great elegance in life. Being tall and broad, she wore her clothes very well, liking strong colours but never looking ostentatious. She wore shirt-waister dresses, jackets, and had a marvellous taste in shoes. Her feet were always elegantly shod.

In the morning, I sat outside to smoke a cigarette whilst my husband and his sisters sat with their mother. She had had a smooth crossing, though very painful at the end. They wanted to talk about her life, so I left them to it. Her garden was small, the dry sandy soil bare in the winter morning. The straight tall trees around it shivered in the cold sunlight. I sat in a white plastic chair, cigarette in my hand and saw her on the other side, in the garden, looking at the light. She came from my right towards the light, a shining smile on her face. She wore a very smart soft grey dress, bloused at the top, with wide sleeves and tight cuffs fastened with four small buttons in Edwardian style. There was a tight belt at her waist and the skirt pencilled to her calves. On her feet were patent black sandals, elegant and extremely high heeled. She ran lightly, aged about mid-20s. Her hair was dark and piled at the back of her head. She was very, very happy, moving swiftly towards the beings of light who moved in waves towards her. In her hands she held a bouquet of marguerites, as though she had just been presented with them, proud and innocent in her pleasure.

The garden was alive with flowers and I stood in it. Whether I was visible to her I don't know. I had a ghostly feeling about my presence there, as though I were a voyeur. And I was quite conscious of sitting in the plastic chair in her garden whilst standing on the other side too. Instantly, I was on both sides of the river at the same time, seeing her running from behind and from the side. I felt quite dizzy, but not unpleasantly, however, as it seemed quite normal to be in both worlds at the same time and therefore also possible to see from all sides at once. On this side of the river, I could see, far in the distance, a small dark woman wearing a heavy coat and a headscarf, toiling up the path to the river. I saw that she could see the light beyond the river, but her main focus was on reaching the dark bank. It was very hard work for her. I did not know who she was, but the contrast between my beaming mother-in-law and the little dark lady was enormous. And the joy in me for my mother-in-law spilled out of me towards the little lady, wanting her to see the joy she was working so hard to meet.

I loved my mother-in-law very much and went through the funeral in a state of happiness for her departing. All the family, though they grieved for her passing and knew they would miss her, were happy for her. We buried her in the forest, a lovely cemetery, and snow fell, a gleaming white powdering like icing sugar, and we put flowers over her grave. The next day, when we visited, the deer had eaten all the flowers, leaving only the stalks. It seemed quite right to have made this offering, knowing that she held living flowers in her hands on the other side.

We went home and began the job of sorting out her belongings. Of course we stopped at the photograph albums, my husband and his sisters looking at the pictures of themselves when they were little, and enjoying the memories. I exclaimed at one photo, because she was wearing her hair exactly as I had seen her. The design of the dress was almost identical, and on her feet were the elegant strap sandals I had seen her wear in the garden. I had not seen that photo before.

I waited to grieve for her passing, but I could not. Somehow, seeing her so happy and expectant before the great light on the other side remained in my memory more than seeing her body in the coffin. It was as though that bit was quite insignificant – the joy of the meeting on the other side was so much more important. I miss her, in many small ways, and think of her often, but I am sure she is going forward with her angel.

An Old Friend Dies

My mother-in-law died in December. In January another old friend crossed over the river. My life with her had been as complicated as it had been wonderful with my mother-in-law. This old lady was often bitter, complained about people's frailties, and was an exacting companion. We had shared a house for seven years and, despite her difficult temperament, had succeeded in building mutual respect and even a good friendship. I had slowly learned to appreciate her. Over the years, she told me about her suffering during the Second World War, her unhappy marriage and the many disappointments she met on her path through life. Her subsequent determination to make a life on her own as an art therapist, bringing light into the lives of people with disabilities, seemed a very fitting road to redressing her own pain. She had one thing in common with my mother-in-law and that was the gift of uncompromising truthfulness. But her manifestation of this quality was all too often hurtful to the recipient of her truths, whereas my mother-in-law could make one see the unpleasant truths for oneself, which is always far less damaging.

For various reasons, my husband and I decided to live in a different community, in order to find a new perspective on life with the disabled. So I rarely saw my elderly friend over a period of seven years. When we returned to our home-base, our friendship had foundered on the rocks of personal problems. I had not been able to retain my friendship with all the members of her family. This she could not forgive and it spoilt things between us. She judged harshly, perhaps truthfully, but without compromise or forgiveness. It seemed best to let things go, not to hold on to what we had had, but to hope for some future redemption. However, such rifts leave scars and I wanted to heal them, so I included her in my nightly prayers, hoping that a new relationship might eventually grow.

At midnight on that New Year's changeover in time, we met face to face. She was ill, dying of lung cancer and exceedingly frail. Through her suffering shone the brightest of light. I was quite overcome and instinctively wanted to kiss her cheek. She pulled back, refusing me, but held out her hand to be shaken, and allowed me to wish her a good New Year. I couldn't say 'happy' because it would have been a lie. Happiness is for living on earth, in a physical body. But goodness can be carried across the river. Six days later she died, quietly and serenely, asking her friend who sat with her to wash her and put on her best blouse and necklace. She lay in her bed and just stopped breathing. A woman who could create a mountain of problems for others passed away without fuss or bother, at the time of her choosing, beautifully prepared for the crossing.

Through all the years of knowing her, she had exasperated me, infuriated me, hurt me, and called up in me the greatest compassion. I admired her for her courage in adversity, and the kindness she could show to others in times of need. Her inner conviction that one could be the director of one's destiny, even when outwardly one was often a victim, had never failed her. I went to see her the same afternoon that she died, feeling a bit afraid because I thought that she would not have wanted me to do so when she was alive. But now, in death, I could finally see her and perhaps make my peace with her. Around her was that peace I sought, contentment and harmony filling her bedroom. I went to the other side, but saw no one, only the garden, alive with flowers, and the surging radiant light.

New Experiences on the Other Side

Because of the course I had started for homemakers I travelled a great deal, offering workshops for communities striving to create homes for people with special needs. A few days after my friend's death, I went to Israel for a workshop. On arrival I heard that the leader of the children's home could not be present at the sessions because his father had died that morning, so we went ahead without him. But that night I saw the black river again. I stood at its shores, on this side, and saw on the other side at the edge of the garden a small black silhouette of a dancing, agonized old man. He seemed to be jumping on hot coals, the way he was leaping up and down, and great confusion poured across to me from him. I was filled with his pain and fear. The light behind seemed to be begging him to turn, but something was holding him to the spot and he could not turn round, only dance in distress. He knew the light was there, but seemed to be prevented from turning into it by something beyond his control. I tried to talk to him, to tell him to turn around, but he could not hear me. I thought: 'This is almost like my friend who drowned. Why is this old man so tormented? Why is he stopped from turning round?'

Then I was here again, but the memory of his disorientation was vivid. I decided to pray for him, even though I did not know who he was. During my prayer, I found myself at the river again and saw my difficult friend who had just died, walking towards the suffering man whose face I still could not see but whose every gesture showed torment. My friend was wearing a thin-coloured skirt, blues and magentas, reds, pinks and torquoises, shaded in the fabric. She wore a cream silk blouse, the collar rounded and scalloped at the edges. It was buttoned up to the neck, the buttons covered with the same silk material. She also wore a thin wool waistcoat, mauve, which blended all the colours well together. She would have been around 50 years old, roughly the age when I first knew her. She wore sandals, creamy in colour, and she came over the greenness of the garden in determination. She called to the old man. He slowed his agonized dancing and brought his hands down from over his head. As soon as he was still, the light behind surged forward and a silvery white flame separated off and moved towards him. A golden flame did the same behind my friend. They turned together, both facing their light. She went forward in her golden glow to the right and the silver flame shepherded the old man towards the left. He walked as though blind and ill, humbly letting himself be guided. The garden glowed and sang and then was empty.

I was quite dazed by this experience. What did these two have in common? I had no doubt now that the man was the father who had died the previous day, but my friend could not have known him in this life. Was I the connection? Was my effort to help him the call to a soul who had just newly crossed over?

Later, I learned that in the Jewish faith one buries the dead as quickly as possible, unlike in the Christian religion where one waits three days. I think those three days are very important. During life on earth, one is attached to one's body, even to the point that some people identify themselves with their physical appearance. After letting it go, it must take some time to get used to being without it.

The man who died was buried that same day, in a concrete wall. Graves in Jerusalem cannot be dug into the rock on which the city is built. So walls are prepared with slots for the corpses. My imagination took me instantly to the narrow, crowded bunks in the concentration camps. The distress of losing one's body and finding it sealed into a wall must be immense. No matter how prepared one is to die, it takes three days to make the change. Butterflies, too, take their time to emerge from the chrysalis.

I was so relieved to know that my friend had come to help the old man. And I wondered about the different light beings, one so silver-white and one so yellow-gold, also that they went in distinctly different directions, one to the right and one to the left.

There must be laws about this in the spirit world. Here on earth, according to folklore, the right signifies the present, the left the past or the future. Do directions have significance over there? And what is their significance? I saw that there is a great deal to be learned, but where could I find the map?

I thought I would try to talk about my experiences, but to whom could I talk? Then I thought that perhaps I should just keep them to myself and be open to learn more. Maybe I will never cross over again, maybe more will be shown to me. But the most important thing is to remain open to whatever might happen.

When the son of the old man came back, we talked about his dying. I did not tell him about seeing his father. But, to my surprise, he asked me what he should do to help, because he felt his father was distressed and shocked. He thought the rapid burial was holding him back. So I said perhaps he should pray for him and help him to see the light.

I knew that the old man would find his way, he had been offered help, but nevertheless I was haunted by the awful gestures and contortions he made when first finding himself on the other side. He was after all an old man and must have known he would die soon. So why the agony?

Witnessing Crossing of the River

Some months later, I woke up one morning and saw a lady in black. She was on the other side of the river, I was on this side, at the edge. She was tall, well dressed, had short black hair, neatly cut. Though I saw her from behind, I could also see her face, white and elegant with bright red lipstick. She gave me the impression of timelessness in her clothing, though it could have been a 1960s old lady's dress. I could not see her shoes. She stood upright, a tall lady, waiting for the light to greet her.

Clearly she could see the light, but made no effort to meet it. Her body language said it would have to come to her. The light glimmered and moved and the garden was a green living lawn, quite empty of flowers but very alive and soft underfoot.

Behind her, on this side of the river, stood a man (also in black). I recognized him to be the father of a friend. I had met him once when he came to see my friend. He looked very anxious and afraid, his head bent, gazing on the black, slow-moving waters of the river. I was standing a little to the right of him, in my usual place. The man would not look up. He could not see the light, or the garden, or the lady on the other side. He was transfixed with fear of the river. I understood that in his view the other side was in pitch-black darkness. In fact, he knew there was no other side and that this was the end. He was afraid to step into the river and drown. He stood, favouring one leg as though in pain from the long walk to the river. The lady on the other side appeared to be waiting for him, as well as for the light.

Then the phone rang and startled me into this morning world. It was my friend, the daughter of the man I had seen at the river's edge. She rang to tell me that her grandmother had died and that her father was very ill and dying. I knew instantly who I had seen and described them to her. She listened, and said that the lady was definitely her grandmother and it would be just like her to wait for the light to come to her, rather than go to it!

Her father had had a difficult life. He was an artist, working for the theatre as a set designer. He was also an alcoholic. I had seen some of his drawings for sets and they were marvellous, satirical, atheist and powerful – and always a little cruel. Now at the end of his life, the drink had completely taken over, he suffered from gout and had developed ulcers on his legs and foot. He had been found in a coma in his filthy flat because his mother, the day before she died, told people to look for him. She said that she knew he was in danger. How right she had been! And what an amazing last call from his angel to hers!

Now he was in hospital and his daughter visited him. He did not really know who she was (he was confused and semi-conscious). The doctors said it could take either a long or a short time till he passed away and so eventually she came home, knowing her prayers would reach him whether she was with him at his bedside or at a distance from him. During the next few weeks I saw him often, at all sorts of odd times. Whether I chose to or not, I would be at the river, urging him to look up, to look at the wonders on the other side. But he didn't − or wouldn't − hear me. He just stared stubbornly at the river, which I began to notice was narrowing every time I went there, getting slimmer and slimmer till it was a stream and then a trickle in a deep crevasse.

I saw also, each time, that the little old lady in a dark green coat and headscarf was some way behind and below him, walking slowly along a winding path towards the river. I recognized her now. She was my mother.

The landscape on this side is hilly, and can be mountainous, and through it winds a narrow path along which the dying walk. For my mother it was still a long way to travel and she was moving quite slowly and peacefully, as though on a Sunday walk. But her face was very serious and intent, as though inwardly she was working very hard.

I realized something new in connection with my friend's father: when a person is dying, I am on this side of the river; and once a person has crossed over, I am on that side with them. But they do not seem to see me. Now I was on both sides at the same time, here with my friend's father and my mother, and there with my friend's grandmother. So I saw everything from all sides at the same time. There is no space on the other side, nor time. All is simultaneity and so I can see someone from behind and face to face at the same time. This may sound disorientating but it is not. It is just how it is.

I began to worry about my friend's father. I could not get him to look up and see that there is life on the other side, vibrant and welcoming, and that his mother is waiting for him too. I tried to tell him, over and over again — but to no avail. Days passed. Then I saw him on both sides at once. On this side he stood as usual, head bent, gaze fixed on the river at his feet, which was now so narrow I could hardly see it. On the other side, standing in the garden, was an identical figure but with one difference. His feet and legs were quite whole and well and he looked younger, head up and very tall.

I said to the man on this side: 'Look, there you are! All you have to do is step over.' And I saw that there was no river any more. And he was on the other side, one with his whole and wholesome self. His mother was gone and he stood alone looking at the light in wonder.

This time I was quick enough to look at the clock in the kitchen. I wasn't any longer so afraid and had my wits all together. The time was 7.55 a.m. I knew he had died and sat waiting for the telephone call. It came ten minutes later. They said he died at 8.10 a.m. I told my friend that I had seen him and how happy he was. She said she knew, because she felt he had been gone a while already, not wanting to live here any more.

Through my friend's father's crossing, I now know how we cross over that black river that lies between this life and the other. The river vanishes at the moment of death. It is simply not there any more. What was once a threshold has closed over and one can step from one firm ground to another. However, again through my friend's father, I saw how long it can take to summon up the courage and the hope for life after life. It *does* take courage, because unless one is sure of the light what else is there to take one across? And the firm ground on the other side looks shifty and vibrant with movement, so how can one know that it is, in reality, a firm foothold? We are so very tied to our physical bodies here in this life that one can only hope for life after life.

I wondered about the time difference. Do we die before we actually stop breathing and are declared dead? Does it depend on how we die, whether suddenly by accident or through a slow long illness? I know the time he died, but they said in the hospital that it was 15 minutes later. Was he alone at that moment of passing and they fixed the time when they found him? Do we cross over before letting go of the body? Or after?

Since the death of my friend's father, crossing over became easy. I just went to the other side whenever I felt the need to do so. This was such an amazing thing that I played with my new-found skill quite recklessly. I set it as a test, in order to prove to myself that my experiences were entirely real. I went every day, sometimes three or four times, just to make the crossing and to see if I could go somewhere else. But I found that I always arrived at the same spot and that I could change nothing. That is to say, I made things appear – people, houses, flowers – and though they came at my bidding, they quickly faded away and the garden returned to its normal state of living green, bright waving light and bordered by a dark river. These visits always took me to the garden on the other side of the river. My place seemed to be to the right just over the river, and my gaze was turned to the light at my right side. Facing me was the expanse of green 'grass' and flowers, and in the distance far along the bank of the river was a blur of shadow that never moved. I did not know what it was or meant.

Across the river was 'the earth' with its hills and mountain, and a path that wound its way to the top of the mountain where the river was situated. Geographically, this is nonsense. Since when does a river, broad, deep and silent, run along the flat top of a mountain. I have seen high mountain lakes, but never a river. However, this is where the river of death runs, along the top of a high mountain.

On all my deliberate visits, I saw my mother, small and darkly clad. Though far in the distance on that winding path, I always saw her face, serious, intent and meditative. My mother has one characteristic mark. She has a stiff leg and walks with a limp. There she was limping up the path, in her dark green winter coat, a dark headscarf on her head. In latter years, she used a walking-stick, but when I saw her on the path she was without it.

Once I had tested my ability to cross over at will, I stopped playing with it. It seemed too precious to mess about with. I also told one or two people about it and no one laughed. They only said I should try to discover why I was given this gift. I felt the same. There had to be a reason. So I limited myself to a look each morning on wakening. I thought that if I was given this gift to help others then I should check each day in case someone was stuck at the river or could not see the light after crossing. But I met no one, and had only a vague feeling of people being there, but none that I could see. The dark shadow in the distance along the river disturbed me a bit, but not enough to want to go and see what was there. It niggled at the back of my mind. But I thought that if it were important I would get there eventually. So far, developments in my orientation on the other side were coming as seemed necessary.

Then my mother became obviously ill. She was approaching 90 years of age, and from being quite remarkably dynamic she became querulous and needy — as well as very yellow. Her companion could no longer care for her needs, being elderly herself. So my husband and I moved into her house and her companion into ours, together with a friend. And I began to look after my mother. I knew she was dying and so did she. The certainty of parting sharpened my consciousness of the finality of death and with it my joy at being able to go over to the other side. Though I knew I would not be able to talk with her once she had gone over, I also knew that I would know where she was and that she would see the light straight away. So my morning ritual of visiting the garden became like a walk in a landscape that I looked forward to each day.

The Death of the Cricketer

Then a famous young cricketer died. I am not normally a sports fan but I had heard about him because he was young and so gifted at his chosen sport. Once or twice I had caught a glimpse of him on the television news. He died in a car crash, suddenly and inexplicably on his way to a party. I heard the news and saw him standing next to the crushed Porsche, calling to his girl-friend, and to the family who were parked in their own car. He knocked on their window and tried to tell them he was with them and fine, but they didn't see him. They saw the wreckage. He saw it too, saw his body, and felt sorry for it. I saw all this in a flash, so fast that I am not sure that I did not imagine it. I am writing about this because I want to make it clear that I am still learning where I meet reality and where my sympathies take over. Seeing the cricketer who died in Australia, near the scene of his death, is an episode I cannot truly vouch for as inner vision.

The next morning I found myself in the garden. It had changed completely. Now it was a cricket pitch, bright lights blazing, and a solitary young man absent-mindedly swinging his bat, obviously waiting for the rest of the team to come onto the field.

As I stood in my usual place, I could see this scene as though with his young eyes. At the same time, I could see the actual garden, and the beings of light calling to the young man in his white cricket flannels. *He* saw the light beings as the bright lights over the cricket pitch, and the garden as the grass field. Round the field he saw the tiers of seats for the watchers of the game. He was quite clearly trapped in his last thoughts of his earth life, oblivious to the fact of his separation from his body, and unable as yet to realize his new consciousness. So he stayed in his happiest moment before crossing over — playing cricket.

For three days I saw him on the cricket pitch and always idly waiting for his team-mates. On the last day he was wandering about, holding his bat and appearing a bit anxious. The tiers of seats were vaguer in outline as though fading, and through them the real garden was becoming more visible. He seemed very lost.

Suddenly, the Queen Mother walked over to him. I was completely startled. I did not yet know that she had died. She was wearing that familiar powder-blue outfit she wore for her last birthday, the hat at its jaunty angle and pearls around her neck. She also had her handbag! And her 1950s shoes. Wonderful! She smiled her elegant warm yet forbidding smile and, holding out her arm to the cricketer, she said: 'Come along now, old chap!' in a cheerful and commanding way. He took her arm, smiling, and walked out of the cricket pitch into the light. He was dazzled and joyous, she calm, serene and clearly expecting to be met. She *knew* where she was, knew that beings were awaiting her. After all, she had been a queen all her life on this side, and was clearly expecting the light beings to welcome her with a red carpet on the other side. A really great soul!

I was sitting outside the house in our back garden, which is a rocky wild-flower garden, full of ferns and wild strawberries in the summer. This was spring, and the daffodils were still out, yellow in the weak sunlight. And there I sat, laughing at the meeting of the cricketer and the Queen Mother. I went back to see them again, right there and then, but they had gone and only the surging of the light beings showed that something momentous had just happened.

The dark river flowed on, my mother was still walking. The garden was as always, except that the cricket pitch was still there but now nearer to the dark shadow in the distance, and less substantial — but clearly still there. For the next few days it remained. Each time I went to look, it became paler in features and smaller in size. Was its presence because the cricketer still remembered it as his most important activity when in his body? Did it take as long to fade away as it took him to forget it?

Why did I see him? The Queen Mother is a famous figure, everyone in Britain having some kind of connection to her. So seeing her on the other side did not really surprise me, except that I saw her before I heard the news of her death. But I have no connection to cricket or to the young man who died so suddenly. Perhaps it was the tragedy of his untimely passing that opened the way to my seeing him. Or maybe it was the great feeling I had for his family, to lose someone so loved so young. I know that at the hearing of his death I experienced an instant and huge fellow-feeling because of the nearness in age of the young man to my son. I felt an agony of loss hitting me. But this is merely sympathy, which I am sure does *not* open the way to the other side. I can find no explanation for meeting him in the garden.

All those days with the cricketer I saw my mother. She was still wearing her coat, but the headscarf was falling back from her forehead and making her face more and more visible. Then I realized that she was a lot closer to the river. I wondered whether I should tell her that I could see her approaching the river. I wondered whether I should tell her anything at all about my visits to the other side. My mother and I had an unusual relationship. On the one hand we were able to talk about almost anything as equals, but on the other hand she could be sceptical of any spiritual insights I reached. She would cluck her tongue and tell me not to intellectualize such things. It made me feel that what I was experiencing offended her in some strange sort of way. So for a long time now I had stopped telling her things about the other side.

Though deeply spiritual, my mother always worried about her understanding of the invisible. She completely accepted the world of spirit, but as she mistrusted her own experiences she chose to turn to those of others whom she deemed truthful. My experiences seemed fanciful to her, perhaps because she knew me as her daughter, knew my temper, my criticisms, my failures, and so could not lift herself above them. We were very close, had a great affection for each other, but real independent respect she withheld from me. So I did not feel able to tell her about what I saw. I kept silent, only telling my sisters, my husband and my friend.

Through my visits to the garden, I followed my mother's progress, hoping that my daily care of her would properly match the stages on the path towards death and another life beyond.

Violent Death

The atrocity of the young suicide bomber who blew up a hotel where a group of elderly people were eating their Passover meal brought me once again to the other side. Now there were people again, in two groups, both very differently occupied. One group was seated around a blanket neatly spread on the living green grass, and on which was laid a lovely picnic. The environment was a city parkland, with benches and rows of trees giving their shade in the brightness of the spirit light, which to those who were partying appeared to be coming from the midday sun in Israel, hot and blinding. Some wore rolled up shirt-sleeves, some wore plastic green sunshades across their foreheads, some wore caps. One woman wore a headscarf, tied in gypsy fashion, her wrinkled brown cheekbones giving her a Slavic appearance. They were happily eating sandwiches and seemed to be waiting for a friend to arrive, impatiently chatting and looking off into the distance towards the shadow that I always saw, away to the left.

The other group were huddled fearfully in a concrete bunker, of the kind one can see at the sea's edge along the British beaches, built during the Second World War to shelter the soldiers on duty against an oncoming invasion. The bright spirit light shone in through the gun slits, and those sitting directly opposite the slits were squinting at its brightness. They clearly knew that a huge explosion has just taken place and were wondering how long they needed to stay in the shelter before venturing out to view the carnage. They wore grey clothes, grey with debris dust, and their fear filled the small space with a smell like rancid sweat.

Outside the bomb shelter the light was moving busily, growing in size and diminishing again, differentiation of angelic beings working with light concentrations to dissolve the concrete. But as fast as an area was thinned to nothingness it closed over again, being woven into reality by the waves of fear from the people inside. Patiently, the light began to dissolve it again.

For three days, each time I visited the garden these two scenes were being played out and I was like an audience of one, watching a rerun of two theatre plays. I stood, as usual, just across the river in the garden to the right, looking down over the scenery towards the dark shadow in the far distance. As I watched the patient work of the light around the bomb shelter, I became aware that the picnic scene had changed in small ways. One of the gentlemen wearing golfing trousers had stood up and had wandered off from the group. He was looking in wonder at a being of light and seemed to be talking to it, as though asking the way. The being enveloped him and he vanished, melted into the light. For the first time I saw how we enter the next stage. We leave our thoughts of our bodies as though they never were, and in that moment we become one with the light – paler and less directed, but created light of the spirit.

The others did not appear to miss him, but they were all getting more restless, sitting straighter, or lounging back and gazing at the bright light that they still imagined was the noon-day sun, apparently wondering why it never moved towards the horizon. They were very anxious.

In the bunker, one woman had begun to look clearly at the light coming through the gun slits, and wore a face of wonder and dawning joy. Over her head, the concrete had thinned to near nothingness and a glorious shaft of light took her by the hand and lifted her out. She was also Slavic in appearance, wearing a long dark blue skirt and white apron. She stood next to her angel and smiled in a dazzling way at the vision of the garden. She thought she was all alone, the only one to be freed, and she grieved for the others.

Each time I visited over the three days, the group at the picnic was smaller. The people who left must have gone when I was not there, because I did not see anyone else leave. They gradually went, and on the third day only the blanket, empty of food, was still in the park that their thoughts had created. They had built a lovely way to adjust themselves to being on the other side, a gentle crossing.

The bunker was another story. The roof was now gone, melted by the loving light, and the few left within were huddled, terri-fied, waiting for what seemed to be a nuclear fall-out. Their terror was almost tangible. The harder the light worked, the more afraid they became, agony distorting their faces. The women had gone, only four men remained. Into my mind came vivid pictures of the gas chambers, of airless choking. I wanted so very much to help them to see where they were, but I could not move from my place in the garden. And the light beings wove busily, waves of warmth and faint music emanating from them.

On my last visit, on day four, the bunker was empty. They had all gone — I hoped into the light and with the light, and no longer afraid. The bunker remained, a ruin of roofless concrete. The picnic area had vanished, the living garden whole once more, marred only by the ugly shelter. It took almost a week to fade (it must have been built with very strong thoughts).

Joining My Mother on the Journey

I had been so preoccupied by the Passover groups that I did not see my mother during those days. I was very conscious of the fact that there had to be a reason for my being there during those old people's crossing, but I could not discover what it was, nor what I should do about it. Though less disturbing than my other witnessing, it did shake me up. And I was so glad to see that they all took only four days to make it into the light.

Now I saw my mother again. She was very close to the river. The path had levelled off and was leading straight to the bank. She still wore her green coat, but her headscarf had almost slipped off. She wore a serious expression, her forehead wrinkled in thought, her eyes vaguely searching for the river, slightly unfocused. She often wore that look in life, when deep in thought or very tired.

I knew now that she would soon die. I did not tell my family at first because I was so overwhelmed. And to tell the honest truth, I was also ashamed. Why I should feel shame I cannot explain, but I did. And I felt that unless I could speak joyfully and clearly about what I was seeing, I should say nothing. On this side, we all knew that my mother was very yellow, that we were getting a hospital appointment for a check-up, to be given a diagnosis, and that she was nearing 90 years. Clearly she was close to dying.

Then I decided that I would cross over every morning to see

how she was getting on with her journey to the other side. But I could not cross. Nothing! I could not even see the garden or the river, let alone the light. I simply stayed here, in my ordinary consciousness. What a shock that was. For over four months I had been crossing, almost at will, and though I could never choose the scenes I saw, I could certainly visit any time I liked. Now everything had closed off.

I felt bereft, angry, disappointed and worried. Had I imagined it all, was I a cheat and a liar? I went into my memory and found that all I had witnessed was true and clear, but now it had stopped, was gone. I could no longer enter the garden whenever I liked.

So I gave up. I left it alone. And I found I was there again, surprisingly, one lunch break as I sat outside in our back garden. I'd been listening to the spring song of the birds and trying to make up my mind to move our household, lock stock and barrel up to my mother's house because she needed me to care for her. There I was, in the living garden in a midsummer light, with roses scenting the air, and my mother standing at the river's edge. The relief and joy in me cannot be described. It was as though I had regained my sight and hearing after a lifetime of blindness and deafness.

Now I understood what had happened. I had *wanted with greedy will* to go to the other side. I had an agenda, one that fed my insecurity and need-to-know. My dirtied purpose had cut me off from the reality of the other side. So I sat on my bench and laughed with relief. There can be no cheating with the spirits on the other side.

But the big question still remained: *why was I given the privilege of seeing?* I did not know. And as I watched over and accompanied my mother's crossing, this question grew and grew in me. I had lived all my life so far knowing that there is always a purpose in the experiences one makes, both outwardly and inwardly. And now I was experiencing a remarkable thing, and could not consciously find its purpose. I resolved to wait, to be happy, to help my mother and her family and friends, and to be open to understanding one day why I had been granted a way over to the other side.

Understanding came only after she had crossed over. Two people whom I spoke to about her dying asked me to write down the journey we made together, my mother and I. The one was an elderly man, who listened to the story and urged me to write every detail of her passing. He said that the way to the other side had been opened to me because I had fully entered into the tiny steps that dying takes, and that I had mostly rejoiced in its progress, rather than wailed over fate, pain and death.

The other person was our priest, who said that so many people who accompany a friend towards death have similar experiences. But their acknowledgement of the events varies so much, either because their environment is unsympathetic, or because they do not trust what they see and hear, putting it down to stress. It would be important, they both said — each on separate occasions — that I write it down. It would allow others to find a meaning in the experiences they too are probably having or have had.

I knew, as they each made their request, that I would have to do what they asked. And I also knew that this would make it all stop. I would be barred from the other side. I must confess I had some moments of regret, a selfish wish that I could keep on crossing over at will because the other side is so utterly life affirming. But one is not permitted to indulge in spiritual experiences. They simply cease if one's motives are impure. I had already observed this when I wanted to cross over with a personal agenda.

So I took up the challenge, and the following pages are a diary of the path my mother and I trod together towards the river — she to cross over, and I to witness her crossing.

Part Two

THE RAINBOW — A DIARY OF MY MOTHER'S DYING

February

My mother phones me. She does this often. There isn't
always a good reason, except my neglect. We live on the
same campus, in a community working with disabled
people. We see each other almost every day. I am often a
bit impatient with her. I know she is old, and I ought to
want to see her daily. But I am busy with my own life and
she has a companion who is her greatest friend. So she
can wait, I think meanly. But she phones, Veronika! She
complains in her Austrian accent, You never visit me. I
think: I visit you every day, every morning on the other
side, but I do not tell her this. She would be annoyed
with me. Instead I say: I'll come and see you today,
later on.

When I get there, we have a lovely chat about nothing,
and I notice that she looks very pale, almost yellow,
and awfully thin and frail. On the other side she looks
serene, here she looks anxious. I feel sorry for my
impatience.

She asks: Why am I still here? I want to say: You're
nearly there! But I don't have the courage.

I remind her that my sister Agnes, and her husband
Huib, will be visiting next week, and she cheers up
immensely. She complains gently that she will miss
Erika, her companion, whose holidays are always
covered by my sister's visits. Isn't it strange how old

people become so dependent on routine? Whenever Erika goes away, my mother gets a little older. Anxiety is aging — must try not to make the same mistake when I am old!

My sister and husband are here. How lovely! We chat as much as we can about everything, including Mother. My sister notes how much she has aged and tells me we must get the doctor to her, she is getting yellower every day. I see her so often I have not really noticed.

The death of an elderly friend last month fills our conversation too. She went so peacefully and without any fuss. I tell my sister about seeing her on the other side, and how she met and guided another soul, the father of a friend. My sister is intrigued. Do I see our mother? Yes, I answer, quite often.

My mother is so very happy. She is a little woman — it's hard to remember we once thought her big and tall! She is frail, has a stiff right leg from childhood TB of the knee joint, but has always (in our memory) had remarkably good health. Now she is tiny, thin, dependent in so many ways. She was always very particular about everything. An improperly set table could make her very disapproving. Meals had to be on time, the house clean and tidy. In her inner life, too, that discipline was there, stern and demanding. She meditated every morning, noon and evening.

She is nearly 90, still disciplined, still getting up at 7.00 a.m., still doing her daily meditations. People visit her. It is a pleasure to sit and talk with her. She listens so well, suggests advice and her eyes see clearly into your soul. I find it both a comfort and a

challenge to be 'seen' by her. She is a very active
person in spirit, now that her body is giving up on her.

She still washes herself and walks the stairs twice a
week for her bath, with which I am allowed to assist
her. What a concession! The first time she tested me at
every turn of the way, ending my ordeal with the
accolade: Veronika, I didn't know you could be so
gentle. Ha! I've had three children, cared for
innumerable disabled children and adults. How dare
she? But I forgive her and laugh about it with Rob, my
husband.

Early March

The other side is calling. I'm visiting every day, the
cricketer, the Queen Mother, the Passover people, what
a time!

On this side, my mother is getting sicker, more
yellow. The doctor says it's jaundice, and that we need
to keep her isolated until tests have been done to
ascertain whether it is of an infectious nature or not.
We know it's old age, and nevertheless take her for
walks when others are at lunch. The weather is
glorious, a spring like no other. She loves the
wheelchair now. What a palaver when it first arrived.
She wouldn't countenance my suggestion to have one, so
I got the doctor to prescribe it. Suddenly she wants it!
Why won't she take any idea from me? I suppose I'll
always be just her youngest, most difficult daughter.
But I too, love the walks. We visit all the corners of
the estate, meeting people and telling them to keep
their distance. Really, we ought to have a leper's
bell, she remarks.

In the house, she still does most things for herself.

When I offer to help, for which I have to arrange the
time as I'm still working a full day and have my husband
to take care of as well as my deaf daughter at weekends,
she refuses, saying she can manage. Thank God she let me
do her baths, after the time she got stuck and Erika,
aged 70, could barely get her out.

Sometimes Erika is away for a weekend. My mother
doesn't tell me ahead (she phones to let me know when
she has already left). I do not like her being alone at
night. What if she falls? She has a 'Help-the-Aged'
button to press, she tells me. Also, someone sleeps
upstairs. But I know she is too proud to call out.

Today she tells me she lay feeling agonizingly
nauseous all night, swallowing her vomit so as not to
disturb the woman upstairs. I am furious with her! Why
doesn't she accept help? Sometimes she will allow me to
be of service, but never the lady who sleeps upstairs.
Why not?

My husband says: Ignore her. Tell her you will sleep
in the house when Erika is away. Now I discover that
every evening she sits alone in her room, no company.
She cannot read as her eyesight is going. Though she can
'see' through one, she cannot read. Also, she has been
hard of hearing for a few years now, so she can only
listen to very loud music. In the evenings, she feels
she will disturb others. So she goes to bed, at 8.00 p.m.
some nights, and then of course she wakes at 4.00 a.m.
and lies impatient for the nurse in the morning.

She has accepted a nurse to wash her when she rises.
This is a great help to me, as she is so fastidious, and
washing herself could take hours. We got this one
through because the woman who will come every morning
is an old friend. She also accepted, after much

protest, that living upstairs couldn't go on. We made
her a beautiful room downstairs in her cottage, a
lovely old house with a beautiful garden. Erika keeps
it so well, loving flowers, especially wild ones. The
bank at the back is a wild natural beauty spot. I love to
sit there on the wooden bench. It's the warmest part,
being sheltered, and sometimes my mother accompanies
me in the bright spring sunshine. We look at the
daffodils. My mother says: How beautiful the earth is!

Erika has come back from her holidays with
bronchitis! She coughs and has a fever. She won't go to
bed, because my mother needs her.

Mid-March

Things are moving very fast. I see my mother looking
serenely at the river. Should I tell her? No, I can't
talk about it except with my husband.

Erika does not recover quickly. This has to stop. I
talk with a friend of them both, who intervenes and
agrees to tell Erika she must retire. She has cared for
my mother faithfully and excellently, but the time has
come for her to care for herself. Mother will need more
and more attention, and Erika should allow herself to
hand it over to me.

My husband says we should move in with my mother — I
cannot go on running two households. I have been doing
it now for a week and it is too much next to a full-time
involvement in our community. I know this is the right
decision. We can exchange houses with Erika (and the
lady who sleeps upstairs). Our house is so little, just
three rooms, that she can retire happily for the rest of

her life. And it is only a few hundred yards away from my
mother's house — they can see each other as often as
they like. Will Erika accept this idea?

My friend speaks to her, she is so very grateful — but
not tactful in telling my mother. She drops the bomb by
saying she can't do the work any more, so I can do it now,
and she wants to move out.

My mother is devastated. She herself has been saying
for weeks that her care is too much for Erika, but she
doesn't like being virtually told that she is too
demanding. They shout at each other. My friend
smoothes them both down. I am very glad I wasn't there!

The next day, my mother is bright yellow! From a
slightly lemon tinge, she is now golden. She feels
nauseous and cannot eat or use the toilet effectively.

I know that I have taken on a full-time job, but I have
my full-time job already — must I give it up? A group of
friends get together with me to discuss the issue. We
decide that all of us can help with bits during the day,
but the move is necessary to stabilize my mother's
lifestyle. My sister-in-law, Frédérique, offers to
help too. How lucky I am to have her living in our
community too. We have been friends for such a long
time, even before we became relatives. Her mother's
recent death is still very close to her and she is
willing to help me. A few other friends of my mother
come forward with offers of help.

I sit down and make a programme of the day, working
around my schedule and meeting my mother's needs,
writing in the names of those who have offered to help.
I am intensely grateful to all of them.

My mother and her companion are oblivious to all this

organizing. We think it will not help them to accept the
necessity of the changes if they know how complicated
it is. They will want to keep things the same rather
than cause trouble to others.

I communicate all these events to my sisters as they
happen. My phone bill must be awful, I dread to see it.
One sister, Agnes, lives in Holland, the other, Liz, in
Australia. But they need to know what is going on. They
applaud the decisions. Both say: Call us if things get
tough. We want to be there when she dies, before she
dies.

We make plans for them to visit, Agnes in April, Liz
will come for six weeks in the summer.

I am so grateful to all those friends who want to
help me. I love my mother very, very much. She has
always been very critical of me. She thinks I have too
much imagination, that I am critical or even cynical
about life and people and that I don't have enough
faith. I have always tried to show her that I am trying
to attain inner discipline, but my temperament makes
me impatient. I always feel as though I cannot please
her. So now I'm a bit nervous of taking on her care.
Will I manage as she wants it? Will I do things well
enough?

I have never looked after an old person. I worry about
this. My husband, my sisters and my sister-in-law tell
me I'll be fine.

All that packing to do. Will I get enough time? What
date shall we fix for moving? Will it ruin my husband's
Easter break? Probably. But he is patience itself,
just says he's dreading moving all my books. Couldn't
we just leave them? We quarrel over that one!

End of March

Things are moving very, very fast. I am now running two
households, but I know it's not for long, so I can cope.
I sleep at home some nights, some nights with my mother.
I go in after breakfast and spend the morning with her.
Thank God for Eva, the nurse who gets her up! I cook her
lunch, go to the office during the rest-hour, come back
for tea, cook my husband's supper at home, spend the
early evening with my mother and the late evening,
after having helped her to bed, with Rob. I feel
divorced!

I see my mother limping along the river bank,
concentration on her face. Is she looking for a good
place to cross?

My mother finally agrees to see a doctor about her
condition. The nausea is what persuades her. She used
to enjoy food, but now everything makes her feel sick.
However, her usual GP is on holiday so she sees a locum.
The doctor says she needs to go to hospital. My mother
comes home and tells me she is not going.

The doctor phones, we talk, she says she has a bed for
her and that it is very important that she go in for
tests. I say I will try to persuade her. My mother is
adamant. She will take an out-patient's appointment
but will not be admitted. I phone the doctor. She says
she will do her best, but it is very unwise.

That evening we talk. My mother says she is quite old
enough to die. It is her decision. She is not in the
least afraid, but she does not want lots of treatment,
pain and people trying to keep her alive. What for?

I find that I agree with her. But doesn't she want to

know what is the cause of her illness? And if we knew, we could treat it and maybe make the dying less arduous? She has always used homoeopathic remedies. Maybe, if we have a diagnosis, we can find a suitable remedy? She agrees with this, but still refuses to be hospitalized. Her homoeopathic doctor can treat her just as well, after an out-patient's visit. What can I say?

So we discuss my impending move and make plans. We arrange for Erika to go for a week's holiday after Easter. She should pack her things before she goes, and choose which household articles she wants to take with her. The other lady living in the house, a young woman, can perhaps help her? I am disappointed to find that she is not very willing.

So I will have to pack up our house, pack up their house and organize everything and everyone. My temper rises, I am very angry, and therefore not very polite to her.

Easter arrives, my deaf, autistic daughter, Helen Barbara, wants all the trimmings as usual. I try to please everyone. I don't think I'm doing a very good job of it! I can feel the anger, roaring away in my gut. But I smile and smile, and try to be friendly. Am I succeeding?

Helen Barbara is very aware of her grandmother. Though my mother has never learned to sign, they love each other and my daughter visits every week for lunch. They smile at each other. Now she knows her grandmother is very ill and tries to help as much as possible. She is very happy that we are going to live together and packs with enjoyment, looking forward to the move. What a relief! She can be so stubborn when she doesn't understand something.

1–9 April

I talk to my sisters, Agnes and Liz. They give me courage, tell me I'm doing all right. I let out some of my spleen to them. They sympathize, tell me to keep my temper and focus on what has to be done. Should they come now? I say I will call them if I think they should come.

We move. What a day! We pack up the house on one day, get some young men and my soon-to-be son-in-law, Tony, and spend all day humping boxes and furniture. The young woman goes out, disappears. My mother's house is dirty. Moving always makes a mess, but this is awful, gobs of dust on every floor in every room! Erika is elderly, the housekeeping was just too much for her. So, as well as moving things, I clean every room so that we can put our things in.

My sister-in-law, Frédérique, takes care of my mother's needs. This means she can just continue her routine as normal whilst we whiz around her. She is incredibly cheerful, enjoying the buzz. I really love my mother a lot. She rises to all occasions. My sister-in-law seems very depressed. Does my mother's nearness to death remind her of her own loss? I have no time to be properly interested in her needs.

I cannot take my cat with me. I give her to a close friend, Siobhán, who lives down the road and who loves cats. Pussy is not at all phased by this. When she was a kitten she related remarkably to Siobhán's elderly ginger tom, Harry. They meet up again now and touch noses! What a comfort that is to me. I love my cat, a

black-and-white gentle sweet creature, very
entertaining, whom we christened Ascension, because
we found her on Ascension Day. Now I leave her and am
sad. But she is so friendly, she would rub up against my
mother, and her balance is so poor, she'd fall down.
Besides, she hates cats! So I say good-bye to her and
let her go to my friend.

We have done it! All in one day. Here we are, and now I
will take my time unpacking and settling in.
Breakfast, after our first night in the cottage, is as
though we've always lived together.

I'm sorry to admit, but I left our little cottage
dirty. Perhaps the lady who is moving in with Erika will
clean it. She wouldn't want her to come home to a dirty
house. I feel very mean about this, but am too stressed
to care. To accomplish a smooth move around my mother,
we had to work fast. We are now under one roof. People
have offered to help me, so I won't have to be tied to my
mother 24 hours a day, and all is well.

We settle into a routine very quickly. Each day I
unpack a little more. The moving in has taken only one
week. Now I just have to unpack the treasure cupboard, a
glass case full of memorabilia.

I take my mother for a walk every day in her chair. She
so loves the spring air and light. We stop at the
chapel, look at the garden. I'll be there soon, she says
cheerfully. Listen to the blackbird's song. What a
beautiful Easter-time!

I am happy and my mother is happy.

No out-patient's appointment — whatever happened to
the National Health Service? It certainly moves very
slowly. But we know my mother is dying, so what else do

we need to know? And the big event of the month is a visit-to-be from one of my mother's oldest friends called Gisela. It will be so lovely to see her. She will be accompanied by a younger woman, a lovely English lady by the name of Judith.

Now my mother takes over and directs my housekeeping! The old tartar has returned in good form. She sets the menus, tells me who shall sit where at the table. Did I make the beds properly, etc? At first it's quite funny, then I get annoyed. We have a row. I promise to do things exactly as she wants them. Please can she trust me a little? We don't talk for an hour. Then I think how galling it must be not to be able to do things in your own house. So I get her out of her chair and slowly up the stairs to inspect my handiwork in the bedrooms. She is delighted and peace is restored!

I must remember that I live in her house, not she in mine.

Periodically, my mother tells me, when I ask her how she wants something done, to ask Erika. Then she remembers and goes quite melancholy. They had such a great friendship going. It's great that Erika can visit her every day. Up the path every evening comes the friend and they chat together. I'm so grateful because it gives me a bit of free time. I promised to have the house tidy by the time her friend Gisela from Scotland arrives. Now I've hung the last pictures, beautiful work by my deaf autistic artist daughter, Helen Barbara. I take my mother round for inspection of the changes, hoping she will like them. She approves but comments that her granddaughter's art is only art in my fond fancy. I hate her for a few moments. How dare she?

But I swallow my anger and say nothing. Art is what you make of it. If she can't see the beauty, others can. My daughter's pictures hang in many people's houses, and you don't buy a painting for a lot of money if you don't appreciate it.

I realize I'm going to have to swallow a great deal. Old people think they can say anything. And of course, so they can. It doesn't do to die a hypocrite!

Suddenly I am enjoying myself. My mother is going to be as horrid, or as nice, or as pathetic as she feels at that moment and I am privileged to accompany her through it all without any barriers between us. What a pleasure! We're going to have good fun together.

Will we always use a tablecloth the way we always did? Will we have napkins as usual? Don't forget to feed the birds! When will you have some time for me? The first questions are easy to say yes to. But the last irritates. If I'm going to do everything the way she wants it, will I ever have time for her?

Now I truly appreciate Erika's devotion. At the age of 70 years she waited on my mother hand and foot and with such good cheer. What a saint! And I'm no saint at all. I cook small delicious meals, all my mother's favourite foods, but she is increasingly more nauseous and can't eat. The food goes in the compost. But Rob enjoys the fact that I'm at home when he gets home in the evenings, instead of out working. So someone is happy. I talk to my sister Agnes. We decide to hassle the doctors a bit more. What can we do to help our mother except get a diagnosis and then decent treatment?

I am so lucky that my daughter Rachel, her partner Tony and their little daughter live so close by. My

granddaughter Elizabeth is a joy in all this. She
visits me every day, seeing her great-grandmother and
smiling at her. Her very babyness cheers me up. I change
her nappy and see how alike the old and the young are,
just different in size.

10 April

I love the spring. Thank God my mother is dying when the
birds are singing and the flowers blooming. It reminds
me of the garden across the river. I visit. It is empty
of people. My mother is at the river, standing still,
serene and concentrated.

She wakes me in the night, yelling. I run downstairs.
She is moaning and saying: Go away, no! no! I soothe her
and she half wakens, then goes to sleep. In the morning
she tells me she dreamed of the Nazis coming to get her
and her brother. She is ashamed to have called out. She
wants the front door locked. It makes her feel safer at
night. I think about the war years she suffered. She
talks about the guilt she feels because, though she
left Austria in 1938, her parents, a brother, and
numerous relatives died in the Holocaust. She says she
feels guilty that she did not try to save them. But what
could she do? I protest. Quietly she says: I could at
least have tried.

There is nothing I can say to that.

11–16 April

Gisela is a lovely lady. She beams with joy, her smile
like the sun. Mother is so happy to see her. Gisela will
sleep with us, her friend in the little cottage with
Erika. Gisela walks with pain, she lives with pain from
a hip operation that went wrong and cannot be righted.

Her friend broke her arm three weeks ago. So now there are three invalids to care for! But it doesn't feel like that at all. The three ladies have such fun together. They read together, have contacted another friend in the locality who takes them out, and they watch videos. (My mother will never do this with me. She says she can't see them properly, nor hear them.) I am amazed at their energy and enjoyment in life. I clean, cook delicious meals, we sit over them, eating and chatting. My mother, still yellow, laughs a lot and loses ten years.

The outing to the 'soup ladies' (a little café, two miles down the road) is an adventure. Getting my mother, stick, chair and all into a tiny Ford Fiesta, with all the other ladies, is very funny, and tragic. We have to lift her in, and out, and I am not going with them. She panics that they will not hold her firmly and might drop her. This is her greatest fear, that she might fall. She has fallen many times in the past year and each time she trembles for days afterwards, though she has never hurt herself at all. She falls like a cat, loose-limbed.

Now I find, standing in the doorway of Gisela's bedroom one night, that we are chatting about dying. She says my mother is not in the least afraid, and how do I find looking after her? I tell her that it is a pleasure, though also very irritating at times as my mother is so particular about details. We laugh together, and I find myself, to my surprise, telling Gisela about the other side. She listens intently, then asks me if I can see my mother? I tell her that I have seen her, and whilst I am talking find myself hovering between the two worlds, neither here nor there. Something is blocking the way.

She asks me whether I have told others about this gift. I have only told my husband, Siobhán, and my sisters. She says why don't I tell others? I realize I cannot do this. Just as I cannot visit the garden with an agenda, such as wanting to see my mother, I also may not speak about it to just anyone. This would be prostituting the gift, and then it will vanish. I know I am forbidden to gossip about it, or to sensationalize it. The knowledge just sits there in my consciousness. Gisela agrees with me, but says she is so very grateful that I told her.

Getting Mother up the stairs to watch the film *Tea with Mussolini* is an ordeal. I have to walk behind her, ready for her to fall at any moment. She stops on each step. I see she is getting weaker by the day. I wonder about the twice-weekly bath. I love helping her. She lies back in the water, scented with lavender, and luxuriates. Her skin is as soft as Elizabeth's. You'd never think she was 90 years old. She has a figure like a girl, slender and shapely. Her hair is only now really grey.

But she is so very yellow, so frail and luminous. And always gracious and grateful. When I dry her feet, crooked from too small shoes as a child, she thanks me. Every time.

Eva introduces the shower to her. We had it built in downstairs for just this moment. Mother is scared! She doesn't want a new experience. But she grits her teeth and endures. She would much prefer the bath, but the stairs have beaten her. Changing lifelong habits is very hard. She looks pale and weary all day and the next. Gisela and friend leave.

Mother is very quiet, then says: That was a last good-bye. Now every friend I meet will be for the last time. I am so very lucky to have so many friends and to have lived such a rich life.

Rich indeed! Two world wars, Hitler's concentration camps, poverty, inspiration, community with friends, caring for the handicapped, marriage, three children, eleven grandchildren, four great-grandchildren, innumerable encounters with all nationalities of the world through her work with the disabled, an MBE, respect and love of hundreds of people. She sits in her room and prays for humanity.

I cook and clean and rush around, and in between am stilled by her warmth and kindness.

17–24 April

The time has come to get organized. I can't continue my work and care for my mother as well. I sit down and make a schedule. I list off rotas for all those kind people who have offered to help because they love my mother. The schedule looks good, allows me to get out to work. I see I have just written how wonderful it is to care for my mother. Well, that's true but it's also horribly binding, and I only get out during her rest hour. One hour after lunch. Not enough time! I need to be alone sometimes, not always at her beck and call. And I like my work outside the home.

People are surprising. By the time I've called up all those helpful volunteers, I am in tears of fury and anger. Sorry, they all say, I can't help at that time. Or: Sorry, don't pin me down. I'll pop in when I have time! Or, from one charming woman: Don't use me so that you can get out. I'll help your mother, but not you!

I sit and sob in the kitchen. If I am frustrated and can't cope, it will rebound on my mother.

Well, dry your tears, woman, and get on with the job. Be grateful if help comes and use the moments to get out. You can do your office work at six in the morning, before she gets up, and during her rest hour. Or — I continue with my deliberations — you can give up your work. Yes, that's what I'll do. Then I can concentrate properly. But it's a hard decision. Still, Mother will be here only for a little time and then I won't have the pleasure of her company in the same way, so I had better enjoy it to the full. I will accept help when offered but I won't ask for more.

My sister-in-law, Frédérique, stays loyal, thank God. She comes every afternoon. Now we are set into a new pattern. We have the most lovely conversations. I don't feel so pressured to get out so perhaps that frees the way for more talking together.

Mother says: I have told so many lies in my life.

I am appalled. My mother is entirely, brutally truthful. She disagrees. She says her innermost thoughts have not always matched her outer actions. She talked spiritual things but didn't always even believe what she was saying!

All those people you helped over the years with excellent advice, I protest. They write to you now, thanking you. You changed their lives!

Yes, she says, but that was a miracle. I hardly ever really knew what I was saying to them, and now I wonder how I dared to give advice. Everyone has to find their own truth, their own way to the truth, and I wonder if I ever really gave the truth.

I sit and listen to her confessions and want to weep. She is undoubtedly the most uncompromisingly truthful person I have met in my life. I would like to be as straight and true.

She says: I know I must get ill in order to let go of life. I love life, but now I'm tired of it. And I can't let go of it. Something will have to help me to go, that's why I'm ill. But I really want to know what my illness is!

We have still not got that out-patient's appointment. I remind her that she refused admission to hospital, which would have given her her answer. She gets impatient and tells me to go.

One side of my mother is so exhalted, and then the other pops out as a fussy old woman. I love her the more for her human frailties!

She says she would like me to read a normal good novel to her. She is tired of philosophy, too old to understand it. So I begin *The Bird in the Tree*, by Elizabeth Goudge. She revels in the lovely Victorian, sensitively rich English language. My mother's first language was German, growing up in the Jewish quarter in Vienna. She heard mainly Yiddish, but spoke only German. She listens with huge concentration and I feel her eyes fixed on me as I read. I get very, very tired. I have to speak exquisitely clearly, slowly and loudly. The strain is terrible. But the lovely language carries us both.

Mother worries about her correspondence — she has a pile of unanswered letters. I offer to be her secretary. One day she will dictate all her answers.

I think she is now very thin. She hardly weighs

anything at all. I can lift her into bed without much effort. She is also getting rather depressed. Waiting for a diagnosis is not good for her. She keeps asking: What am I dying of?

Sometimes she is confused, and wets herself. She wears nappies at night but uses the toilet during the day. Now it takes her so long to walk to it that accidents happen. So at last she allows me to help her. I marvel at her humbleness, now that she has to give in to my care. She says: What must be, must be. Once I was a baby and needed care. Now I am old and need care once more. Thank you, Veronika.

Her gratitude makes me ashamed of my impatience. But I know I'll get cross with her again and again, because I am so tired. I can't leave her alone at all. And my sister-in-law seems to be depressed. She looks grey sometimes, and I don't know how to cheer her up. I'm too tired to be constantly grateful for every little bit of help given. Why can't people just get on with helping me and I'll thank them when it's all over? I have no time for false sentimentality at the moment, my mother is dying!

The comfort of the other side seems to be fading. I can't see her, except when I'm not expecting it. Then I am there again, in the garden, flowers blooming and the light so radiant. On those days I am less impatient with everyone.

The greatest pleasure is my granddaughter's visits. She laughs and chatters, every day a new development. She grows in beauty and fun. My daughter Rachel and her partner Tony always have something nice to say. And they listen to my grumbling and sympathize.

Elizabeth comes to sleep every morning whilst her

mother works. I take the little warm bundle upstairs and put her to bed. It fills my morning with light to have the young and old together. I am a lucky woman to have so many different experiences. My husband brings warmth and stability. He is at home in the evenings so I can go out. How dare I complain?

Erika visits every evening. She and my mother sit and knit baby clothes, and chat. Our neighbours pop in regularly. My mother loves them. They stay and talk. Did I say no one helps? What a lie, so many people are here for my mother. A small voice says mockingly: They come for your mother, not to help you. I tell it to shut up, I don't need help. What a selfish bitch I am. Rob and Rachel comfort me. They say I am doing all right.

I think it is time to assume that my mother is jaundiced and get some help. Even I can diagnose that! The two community doctors take turns to visit mother, and so we now have a battery of homoeopathic remedies as well as special herb teas. They certainly help the nausea, but she is as yellow as ever.

The worst is the itching. She has started to be tormented by it, all over her body. This prevents her sleeping. We ask for help, Piriton is prescribed. My mother tries it once but can't bear the drowsiness it causes. She doesn't want to go out and meet people when drugged. So she chooses the itching and consciousness, and I say hard-heartedly that I don't want to hear her complain about it if she won't take the cure!

We still take a walk each day, and it seems she says good-bye to another part of our beautiful estate on each occasion.

Looking at the world through the eyes of the dying is a

revelation. Every flower and tree, every raindrop and puff of wind becomes a source of delight. I realize I've never really seen the world until now.

The telephone is both a boon and a curse. I have to keep my sisters up to date. Sometimes I'm so glad to talk to them, other times I just don't want to tell them anything. But I must keep them informed.

Dear Helen Barbara. Patiently she helps with the cleaning and washes dishes, and paints beautiful pictures. She sees her grandmother dying and is quiet and good. I am neglecting her dreadfully.

This will never do. I'm starting to feel sorry for myself. All that consideration for others is just an excuse to feel sorry for myself!

There is a beautiful garden on the other side. The light is the bright surge of love. My mother is crossing and I have seen where she is going. That is the joy on which I should focus.

25–31 April

This is a bad weekend. I have to fulfil an obligation to do a workshop with a group of people in Switzerland. Shall I go and leave mother? She's not dead yet, still makes her bed, tries to wash herself with the help of the nurse, and still wants to have books read to her. She sits patiently and passes the time knitting baby clothes for the newest great-grandchild.

Agnes decides to come so that I can go. Oh, what a relief! I realize I am a bit stir crazy. I need a break. So I go and have a wonderful, stimulating experience.

Am back and hear all the news. Not only Agnes but David, her son, and my son Marty have been to visit. They give Mother lots of attention. She is exhausted but very happy. Agnes, she says, is such a good daughter. And David, she says, has given her the possibility for wonderful talks. She does not mention Marty very much except to say he is very well and doing what he wants to do as a pilot in the military. She says he is doing the right thing for his destiny. I am amazed at her broad-mindedness.

Hurrah! The date for the scan has arrived. We agree that Agnes (the good daughter!) and Eva, the nurse, will take her. Mother wants her daughter present but, when the moment comes, she sends her away and goes with Eva! Why on earth does she blow so hot and cold? Is she trying to spare us what we already know? That's not like her at all. We have always been brutally frank with each other in our family. Maybe she is a bit frightened after all.

The diagnosis is a blockage of the bile duct, probably cancer. So what's new? They refuse to say anything more definite. They want another scan before committing themselves. I think this is a great cover-up.

Mother stands in the doorway of sitting-room and kitchen (a favourite place of hers so no one can go in or out). We tease her about this, then she says: I always knew I would need something to help me to die, but I never thought it would be cancer.

I ask her if she is afraid. She says: No, not of the dying, but of the possible pain. I am not good with pain. Promise me you will not let the pain get too great.

We talk about pain-killers, and decide we will give them to her when she needs them. Does she feel pain now?

No, she says, no pain, only discomfort and terrible nausea and itching. The itching is the worst, it prevents her from sleeping.

Agnes will leave tonight, but first they both want to hear about my exploits in Switzerland. We sit in my mother's beautiful white room and I tell of the exhalted personages who did not recognize my existence until after I had given my presentation. The audience was moved to tears. Then the high and mighty spoke to me, inviting me back next year! My mother wants the content of the presentation, so I tell her about talking with the guardian angel. She listens intently and says: You were right to point out that everyone can talk with angels, that they even do so without recognizing it. That is why the audience wept.

My sister talks to me afterwards in the kitchen. She knows that I don't believe our mother thinks much of my efforts and knowledge. She says I should see Mother's face when I tell her what I am doing. My life's work is to promote a new and true way of homemaking, one that works from a spiritual source and helps the homemaker to see the precious task she has taken on to build the foundations of a wholesome society. The human race will create a dysfunctional society in the future if we cannot re-create a wholesome, healthy home for our children. She reminds me of the home our mother made for us.

I see now that I am more than privileged to make a warm home for my mother through her dying at the end of her life. I can give to her what once she gave to me. We have come full circle.

I love my sister very much, she is so clear sighted!

1 May

Bad day. Mother is deeply depressed. She wants to talk about her condition. She says she feels her body as a great burden and wants to be rid of it.

She feels she is a burden to me and to others. I tell her she is only a burden when she thinks she is. That makes it hard to care for her.

I enjoy being with her, talking with her, reading to her, cooking and cleaning. I have given up work so that I can care properly for her. I tell her my husband loves it because I am always at home and the meals are delicious and on time. For once, he says, I practise what I preach, real homemaking. Doesn't she see that she is giving me a great opportunity?

She laughs a bit and cheers up. But it is so very unlike her to be anything less than positive. I want to take her out, the weather is glorious. She refuses, being too tired. She says she wants to see her GP and homoeopathic doctor together and they shall tell her exactly what is wrong with her. No more lies, or insinuations. She wants to prepare herself for the crossing consciously.

2 May

I ask my mother whether she is really ready to hear about her condition. She says: If I do not ask outright, please do it for me. But let us see if they will tell me the truth first.

Her GP and the other doctor arrive. They talk to Mother gently, hinting at this and that. The GP explains the scan and how it works and what they think they have found: a small obstruction at the mouth of the bile duct. This means the bile goes straight into her bloodstream rather than through the digestive organs, so she cannot digest her food, especially fats, and this makes her nauseous. The yellow colour is because the bile is shooting round in her blood. This is the cause of the itching. He refuses to make any further diagnosis about the blockage, though he admits it is probably cancer.

Mother asks no more, so I ask for her the question she wants answered. Is there any treatment that will ease the discomfort, and that her frail condition will allow? I say that she does not want to prolong her life, only to be perhaps more comfortable until the end. And when will the end be? How long does she have to live? He suggests a by-pass, a relatively simple operation, which she could well undergo in her present state of health. But it would mean being hospitalized and she has refused this. As to how long she still has to live, he would not like to say, but perhaps anything up to six months, depending on whether she will have the by-pass, or not.

She says she will think about it.

3 May

We spent all day yesterday discussing the pros and cons of an operation. Mother in hospital is a weird thought. She depends so much on order and beauty around her. She makes her bed perfectly, smoothes the covers, has fresh flowers on her coffee table. On her bedside table lie her bible, her alarm-clock, and a photograph of my father who died 23 years ago. She looks at it every night before sleeping. Her chair is covered with a sheepskin for warmth as well as homeliness. On her bedroom walls hang pictures of great artists. On the windowsill outside stands a flower-box with seasonal blooms, which she gazes at with love. Beauty, cleanliness and culture surround her.

Her childhood was bleak and deprived of beauty, art and culture. It means so much to her now, to feel her books as her friends and teachers, and to live amongst elegance and style.

In hospital she will have to go with the flow. She will no longer be 'her majesty' whose friends are also her vassals! I cannot imagine she will cope. But she tells me she must endure it. I promise not to leave her alone. She is so afraid of not understanding the nurses and doctors, of losing her autonomy, of becoming a cypher. But she also wants most desperately to have a clear diagnosis. She needs to know exactly and precisely what is killing her, but even more how long it will take.

Agnes and I talk over the phone. We know she will suffer a lot in hospital, but we agree that it has to be done. Am I pushing her into this decision? My sisters, Agnes and Liz, say I am not. I should get it organized.

When should I get Liz over from Australia? I cannot answer this question yet. Mother is depressed but not more ill.

4 May

Friends come as always at 8.30 a.m. to read to the nature spirits. My mother learned from Rudolf Steiner that apart from angelic beings there are also beings who live within nature, within rocks and earth, within plants and water, within air and light, and within fire and warmth. These beings are the guardians of nature. According to Rudolf Steiner, they are both shy of humans and drawn to them. Therefore, when we plough and till, build and make, mine and delve, we disturb them. My mother firmly believes that our inner attitude affects their work. If we do not care about them, they flee, and leave nature to us humans to nurture, which she thinks we don't always do very well! She is such a follower of Steiner that she decided to read specially written verses, which he wrote in the nature of prayers, that exhort nature spirits and human beings to work together. With this, she endeavours to bring back the guardians of our beautiful natural planet earth. As such activity is more powerful when carried out by a group of people, my mother found friends to help her. They have been doing this with my mother for years, every Saturday, under the oak tree along the path to her cottage, to keep the spirits from deserting our lovely farm, fields and woods and garden. I must say that around us nature seems particularly fertile. Flowers bloom around my mother's house earlier and brighter than over the rest of the estate. Perhaps it works?

Today my mother cannot join them. She has had a bad night. So they read outside her bedroom window, and she sits in her chair and contemplates the universe. I sit with her and am taken by the peace that fills her soul when she meditates. She looks quite radiant.

Mother asks for Liz, my sister in Australia. The time has come to call her. Mother does not really believe she will come. To her, born before the First World War, Australia is on another planet. No one returns once they have travelled there! I tell my mother Liz will come soon. She looks sceptical, but a bit more cheerful. I want my daughters with me when I die, she says quietly.

5 May

Mother's Sunday routine never varies. She rises early, puts on her best clothes, has a white roll for breakfast, makes her bed and goes to the service. Today, as I wheel her down to the chapel, we are both aware that it is probably her last service. She can hardly walk into the chapel to her seat in the centre front row. It takes two of us to help her, but she refuses to be wheeled in. She will walk, she declares.

I sit next to her and want to cry. Her face is stern, a crease over her forehead as she follows the words by heart. I know she can no longer hear them all.

On the way home she regrets that she has not got the strength to go to the communion service any more. I suggest the priest may bring the communion to her. This cheers her up a great deal.

6 May

I call the GP again. It's amazing how slowly the wheels of the National Health Service move. Mother has been very ill for two months now and there has been no diagnosis yet, only speculation. I know she has cancer, but how can the doctors just let things ride like this? Is it because she is so old? Is that fair? I am really quite cross and try not to let it show. Mother has the old-fashioned view of doctors. They are like God and one must trust them absolutely. The GP says he will hurry things up.

Mother is very sleepy and quiet today, she seems to be drifting away. I go to the garden but cannot see her.

The river bank is empty. Why can't I see her? I need the comfort too much, perhaps, and my job is here on this side, to help her crossing as properly as I can.

She sits in her chair, dozing, not even knitting, her hands folded over the red scarf she is making for her oldest great-grandchild. I go about my daily chores feeling harassed and ill at ease. I will miss her when she is gone, but right now I find it all a great burden.

7 May

The hospital calls. I should bring her in straight away. I stall them. Now it's going a bit fast! She is old and can't jump to things, she needs adjustment. They say, today or not at all — I can bring her any time before 7.00 p.m. Goodness me! Now it's my fault that she isn't under their care. I feel rather cross, and anxious.

Mother reacts with controlled panic. She is very afraid of the change, afraid of new faces, a new situation. She says she had enough of hospitals when she was a child with TB. But we pack anyway. She tells me what to put in the bag. Her knitting, her bible, her book of meditations, her letters that we will pass the time in answering, her hearing-aid batteries, her blue shawl, her pretty dressing gown and nicest nighties, her washing things and underwear.

She also packs the photograph of my father. She wants it by her bed. She says she will miss it. It is a beloved companion. We talk a bit about his death, so sudden, of a heart attack. I wonder if she envies him his quick crossing, but I do not say this out loud. We have a lengthy discussion over her night nappies. We decide they will surely have them there and don't pack them.

We name-tag her Zimmer. She says: Write Mrs Lipsker
MBE. Then they'll know who I am!

We laugh a lot.

Her homoeopathic doctor visits. I leave them to talk.
She is, after all, also a friend. I feel like my
mother's mother, not her daughter.

Erika and Frédérique come up to the house and we make
up a sort of rota to be with Mother all the time. I cannot
do this alone, I need some help. They are wonderfully
understanding.

My mother calls me in. She makes me promise never to
leave her alone. I see her for the first time, as she
really looks, not as I see her in my mind's eye. She is
very small, frail and yellow. Her shoulders are bowed,
her hands stiff and her hair pale grey, very thin and
fine. She looks like a wrinkled, yellow old crone. Pity
and love for her swell in my throat.

Eva comes to drive her to the hospital. We fold up her
chair, shove her bags in, and help her to be seated. She
is very quiet, like frightened child.

The hospital is awful! I know I should be grateful, I
tell my husband later that night, but I can hardly bear
to leave her there! First, the smell, of old pee and
dying bodies. Then the colours, grey and dark blue.
The neon lights and the sound of the television. The
day room is an open space between the wards, and people
shuffle to and fro or just sit. My mother is given a
bed, very high in the far corner of a six-bed space.
Blankets and sheets! All her life, Mother has slept
under a feather duvet. How will this be, with sheets
and one light-blue polycotton blanket?

She sits patiently whilst the nurse admits her.

Endless questions to which she says: Pardon? She can't follow the Northern Irish accent. I think, too, that she has switched off. I answer them all. Half-way through she rouses herself and says crossly: I am not a baby, I can answer for myself.

I shut up and let the misunderstandings begin. The nurse is impatient but kind. After a few repeats of things she says: I should be off duty, I cannot take so long. Please let your daughter answer.

My mother sulks. I give all the information.

Next to my mother's bed lies a thin, sour-faced old lady. She says, once the nurse has gone: I'm the longest stayer in this ward. If you want to know anything, just ask me. I realize by the severity of her tone that there is a pecking order and that my mother will now be at the bottom! How will that pan out, I wonder, and grin to myself. Mother has been queen of our community all her life. If it comes to a show-down between these two ladies, who will win? I look at my mother and think, she will lose. She has no more will to live and is like a fish out of water.

I help her undress, behind the curtain. She hurries me in case someone should see her naked or, oh shame! in her nappies. The bed is hard, she looks like a tiny mouse in it. I tell the nurse she has never had blankets. She says we can bring up her duvet if it will make her more comfortable. Suddenly I see how kind they all are. And how busy. Only two to a ward of 24 elderly dying women! They are so grateful that I will be there to attend to my mother. One less for them to worry about.

Rob comes with her duvet. She sighs with relief and looks happier. I tuck her in, leave her hearing-aid and glasses where she can find them, and ask if she wants her teeth in a glass of water. No, she says, I will keep them in. (Oh, vanity!)

It cheers me up. There is some spark of resistance in her still, if she cares about her appearance.

We kiss her good night and I promise to be there to help her after breakfast. The nurses will help her to wash and dress and eat her breakfast. She clutches at me: will someone steal her hearing-aids and glasses? I tell her no one wants them, they all have their own. She laughs.

I look back and see her staring at the ceiling, a mouse in a hospital bed. Her Zimmer stands to hand, her wheelchair at the foot of her bed, all tagged.

It's odd to be sitting here in the kitchen at home without her, going to bed without her in the bedroom beneath me, without hearing her breathing and groaning occasionally, without her voice calling me.

Someone once said to me that when one is most spiritually active, then the biggest temptation to darkness of soul will arise. Does accompanying someone to their death, the crossing from one life to another, mean one is spiritually active? I feel totally worn out, used up and fragile most of the time.

So I turn to my friends and family, to those people who love my mother, for help and support. How surprising are their differing responses! My sisters phone and are ready to come whenever I call. Agnes has been twice already and Liz is on her way, knowing her longed for holiday will be cancelled.

Frédérique comes every day, in the afternoons, to

give me a couple of hours to myself for cleaning the
house, which I need, but she also says she needs to see
to it that she does not over-commit herself. She still
is very frail from caring for her own mother until her
death. Others who have committed themselves to being
with my mother cannot seem to find the right moment, the
right time to be with her within their very busy
schedules.

Now that Mother is in hospital, someone has to be with
her all the time. Will this mean I can never have a
moment for myself? Will I too be admitted to hospital
with her? I make a new schedule and ask those friends to
sit with my mother for a few hours every afternoon in a
rota. One by one they explain how they cannot afford the
time. One is angry, writes a horrible letter
describing how selfish I am that I do not want to take
real care of my mother.

I feel sick. Am I really so awful? Then I feel
enormously angry. She is my mother, I do want to care
for her, but how can I do it really well and patiently
when I get no respite?

Next I am shocked at my anger, my almost hatred
towards my friends. I take a long hard look at my
motives, and my needs. I cannot tell my husband
everything about people's reactions to my cry for
help. I tell him about those with the busy schedules,
but I don't tell him about the horrid letter. The woman
who wrote it has been coming for years now, to read to my
mother twice a week. She has never liked me very much,
so perhaps she thinks I want her help in order to help
me. Indeed, why should she help me, if she doesn't like
me? So I write her a letter, saying that whatever she
may think of me is irrelevant, but could she please

continue to spend time with my mother, who so
appreciates it? I will make myself scarce so that she
need not meet me at all. This finds her approval.

So one person can be counted on for help. Erika is
unfailingly willing, that makes number two.
Frédérique does her best, but her troubled state of
mind must be considered. Our neighbours are great. I
shall count my blessings! But in practice I realize I
have to do this all the way, with no excuses and no time
to be tired.

How I hate hospitals, and how much I have to fight with
my anger.

My greatest blessing is a friend who comes every day
for half an hour at ten o'clock, to have a coffee and
smoke a cigarette. All the time my mother was at home, I
could count on that half hour to get out, go for a walk,
fetch the post, sit and chat, whatever I needed to
restore my patience and calmness for the needs that
might follow throughout the rest of the day. Quiet,
unassuming friends are gold dust. She doesn't want
anything, she is simply there.

Now my mother is in hospital, I have the nights to
sleep and I do so, like one dead (forgive the joke,
Mother dear!). I have time to talk to my husband, after
I have got everything ready for the next day's vigil.

I will fight with my demons after Mother has gone. Now
is not the time. But I find I can no longer meet the eyes
of those who have fallen down in my planning.

8–11 May

Liz will arrive on the 11th. Oh, joy! Mother sighs with
relief and pleasure. She does not quite believe it and

periodically smiles when she remembers the news. She is like a small child waiting for her birthday.

Meanwhile, life is pretty awful for her. I came in on the first morning to find her wearing her vest back-to-front on the outside of her nightie. It's got long sleeves, like a fine woollen pullover, so one could be forgiven for thinking that it is one. She is sitting in her chair, shivering without her shawl, her stiff leg unsupported. I ask her who helped her get dressed. She cries small, slow tears. She could not understand the nurses, they do not have the nappies she likes, they did not wash her properly and now she has soiled herself and does not dare to call for help. She has been waiting for me since 7 o'clock!

I take her to the bathroom, feeling terrible. There is no bathroom to soothe her, it is a square room with a toilet and a shower. I swallow my despair, strip her down cheerfully, and wash her with her favourite soap. She keeps asking me to take her to the bathroom, although we are in it! I give up trying to soothe her. She is frightened and confused.

Now back in her chair, with shawl and a leg-support, she sits for a moment, then says: They are really very kind, but they don't understand what I need and they are so busy.

I make a mental note to bring in everything she requires, nappies and all. I vow to be with her all the time. The nurses are a bit impatient with me when I ask for a bath for my mother. Baths happen twice a week and this is not a bath day!

Breakfast is a disaster. She will not eat, only sips some skimmed milk. She says it tastes horrible. What will lunch be like? For the past week she has only eaten soup. No soup, says the dietician. It is not soup day. However, the nurses will kindly make up a Cup o' Soup in the ward kitchen. Good God! Can one get nourished by instant soup? Unfortunately I say this out loud. The dietician is offended. It is full of nutrients, she says stiffly.

I am beginning to feel as bad as my mother. I want to take her home as quickly as possible. I will not let her die here.

Next comes the physiotherapist. She makes my mother walk with her Zimmer. She teaches her, as though she is a baby. She talks to her in very loud baby talk, as though she were an idiot. When my mother is finally allowed to sit down, she says: In here one must give up dignity and independence, one must accept, simply accept. Mother looks like a little reproved schoolgirl, being punished for a crime she does not know she has committed.

The anger bursts out of me. I accost the physio and tell her my mother is neither demented nor mentally deficient. She is merely old, and has used her Zimmer for two years now. Moreover, though she is deaf, and a foreigner, her English is excellent.

Not surprisingly, the physio is offended. I have to endure a telling-off from her superior. But it was worth it because now she speaks properly to my mother, and is helpful with exercising her legs.

Oh, dear, I fear we are not the most popular clients here!

Thank God for my mobile. My husband insisted I take it. Now, when I know my mother will be all right on her own for a few moments, I can get outside for a smoke and talk to Rob. We make plans about food, rest and care.

Lunch sees no soup, but peas, mashed potatoes and chicken. It looks like mud! Mother doesn't eat. Supper is custard and jelly. She doesn't eat. But she drinks her tea, which I fill half full with skimmed milk.

Evening wash is like the morning. As soon as we get into the bathroom (minus bath) she asks me to take her to her bathroom. The confusion is there all over again. I wash her as best as I can and put on her own nappies. I settle her in the big bed and stay for a while, reading to her. She is more peaceful and I am ready to cry.

Frédérique tries to give her some soup the next day. I have made it the night before, putting it in a thermos. From now on I bring in food for her, with a china dish and silver cutlery, and a proper napkin. She enjoys the picnic, laughs and thanks me. She still, however, will not eat. Now Frédérique tries, but Mother politely refuses. That evening I ask Frédérique how it went and say, despairingly: She won't eat for anyone but me, because none of you are bossy enough! This hurts my almost last helper. I see her flinch and know it was the worst thing I could have said to someone who is doing more than their best to help me. Now I realize I will have to do this all alone. I am too scratchy and tired to be tactful any more, I have offended just about everyone. I phone my sister Agnes and cry. Not much help, but at least I sleep well.

My mother has been in hospital for two days and not a test has been done. Apart from admission, no doctor has been. I wonder if they are going to do anything at all? Thursday brings the consultant. My mother sits still, silent, staring blindly in front of her, whilst he talks to me.

She says: I am still here, talk to me, please.

He kneels down and shouts in her ear. She understands nothing. Eventually, I talk to him outside. He says he will hurry up the scan but has to find a free slot in the schedule! Only then will they be able to think about by-passes or not. What can I say?

My mother says: They will do nothing, they cannot do anything, but we must be patient. Her resignation is depressing.

I begin to be her secretary. At home I had no time between cooking, cleaning and so forth. Now I have all day. She lists off all those people she wants to write to, and then we start. Her dictation is faultless, at just the right speed, with punctuation included. Once, when we were interrupted, she continued the sentence as we had left off those five minutes before! Amazing. So she is certainly not dotty, but very depressed. The letters cheer her up, however. She enjoys thinking about her friends and each letter ends with a good-bye.

Whenever I come back in, after a cigarette break (my smoking is mounting), I see that the other lady beside her has tried to start up a conversation. My mother smiles vaguely at her and confides to me that she can't understand a word she says. To be deaf, almost blind and physically disabled puts one in a prison. This period in my mother's life is aging her hourly.

I go on reading to her and she wakes up again, her interest quickened. She enjoys anything that makes her forget where she is. The lack of a bath, the long walk to the toilet, the uncomfortable chair in which she sits, fade out of her awareness whilst I read.

Today her itching is awful. She cannot stop
scratching. They offer her Piriton. She accepts.
Consequently she behaves like an Alzheimer's
sufferer. I cannot read to her, she is confused and will
not eat. She soils herself too.

I talk to Agnes that night. Is this tolerable? Should
we put her through this? Are we right to expect a
possibly impossible by-pass? No one will treat her,
she is fading hourly! We agree I should tackle the
consultant again. My sister says I need to make all the
decisions for our mother. We cannot ask her to make them
herself any more. I struggle with this idea. I still
think she should have some say in how she passes the
rest of her time on earth, but I agree that I will have to
do all the practical thinking.

Tonight she wants a bed-time story. By now we have
evolved a morning and evening ritual of washing,
dressing and feeding. So she lies as comfortably as I
can make her in the huge bed, smiles sweetly and says:
Tell me a story.

What would you like to hear, I ask?

A fairy-tale, perhaps 'Rapunzel', she says eagerly.

All her attention is back in focus! This is
wonderful. So I tell her to put back her hearing-aid.
She doesn't want to do this, says she can hear me
perfectly. She fixes her eyes on my face expectantly,
like a little child. I am so very touched by her
innocence and wisdom, all wrapped up together in this
shrivelled little old body.

So I fold my hands and tell her a fairy-tale, each
night a different one, going through the all-time
favourites, having to read them up in *Grimm's Fairy-*

tales the night before. I love these last moments of intimacy and feel that some of the care she gave me as a child I can now return to her.

The stories bring her peace. She yields herself to the archetypal images that reoccur — the princess, the prince, the witch, the dragon, the wise and the foolish characters that people them.

These are the best times, the worst are the meals. I cook everything for her and bring it up in thermos flasks — she will not touch the hospital food. But she doesn't eat my home cooking either. She is fading away, can hardly walk or talk, needs her wheelchair for every move. She can still just about stand for a wash.

Liz has arrived, oh joy! all the way from Australia. Mother radiates her pleasure and seems to come back to us a bit. She asks after all her family and listens eagerly to the answers, but tires very quickly.

I, too, am relieved. Now I can share the work and responsibility of decisions with someone who can really help.

12–13 May

Liz has her birthday, but we miss out on celebrating — we are too busy. We work out a rota so that each of us can get a break and Mother can enjoy Liz. Another great boon is the fact that Liz can drive. I have always had to arrange a lift, but now Liz drives me or herself. Moreover, Mother eats for Liz, her gentleness a much better sauce than my astringent ways.

Eva has agreed to come in every morning to wash Mother. This means she is much cleaner and more comfortable too. Her self-esteem rises. How important it is, even when busy dying, to care properly for the body. You might be leaving it but, whilst you are still in it, it needs respect! My mother enjoys the care and eats a bit better.

She wants the priest to give her communion. He comes to the hospital and we leave her with him. Afterwards she is quiet, reflective and calm.

In all her weakness she is never-failingly polite and grateful. The nurses love her, especially the night staff. They say she is a real lady. I can't understand a word they say, says my mother, but they are all so kind!

Now her friends start to want to visit her. They know she will soon cross and want a last word from her. A queue forms. We think we need to protect her, but also that the stimulation is good. We ration them day by day.

It is wonderful, says my mother, how many friends I have. I am so grateful that I could give them something in my life. She marvels at this, and then, as I tuck her up in bed that night, she says: 'Tell me a story.' When I have finished recounting the tale of 'Cinderella', she says mischievously: 'I wonder if all the other children in the ward also get a bed-time story?'

14–15 May

At last the scan! It is Liz's turn to be with Mother so she goes with her. The results are the same, a blockage of the bile duct, of unnamed origin. We are told we will have to wait till the consultant comes to decide what next.

16 May

The consultant comes and talks to me as though my mother is not in the room. I ask him to squat down to her ear level and speak quietly, directly to her. He is very good and does this. She nods in comprehension as he says he can get a by-pass done but must first find a hospital with a free slot and the necessary equipment. He will make it as fast as he can. Meanwhile, he recommends that she stay in hospital where she can get the best care. She says with determination: I will not die in hospital!

Now I know that this decision to remain in hospital is wrong. She is far too weak to be operated on, whatever he may say to give us hope. I ask my mother what she wants. She says miserably: I don't want to be kept alive, and I do not want to die in hospital.

My sisters and I discuss the issue. We can all see that she is fading fast and we know what she wants. We do not believe this 'little op', as the doctors call it, will achieve anything, nor that she can really take it. She wants to die at home. No one will, or can, give a clear diagnosis, but it is pretty clear that she is dying.

The consultant refuses to say she has cancer. I suspect he is not telling us the whole truth so as not to upset us, but it has the opposite effect on my mother. She really needs the truth so that she can prepare herself for the crossing. Mother sits slumped in the plastic hospital chair, depressed and silently sinking.

Suddenly I am in the garden. I see her standing at the very narrow river. She is small and upright in form and through her soars a pillar of bright white light as high as eternity. Her face is up-turned and shining.

I know what we must do now.

I call the consultant and explain that my mother wants the last unction and it has to be administered at home. He makes me promise that I will bring her back on Monday, then I can take her home for the weekend. I say that I will do this, but if she refuses to come back I will let them know in good time.

Mother is quite passive. She shows no joy at the thought of going home. Her demeanor here on this side is so very different from the shining strength on the other side. I ask her cruelly whether she wants to come home or die in hospital.

No, she says strongly, all of a sudden roused. *I will not die in hospital*. And her voice has that commanding bite that we used to hear when we were naughty children.

17 May

Mother comes home. I have stayed back this morning and prepared her room. Someone has brought in some branches of azaleas, yellow and scented. Her chair is ready, her bed turned down.

She has to be wheeled from the car to her room, only a few yards. We unpack her things, putting everything back exactly where they belong, the photograph of my father looking as comfortable on her bedside table as she looks in her very own easy chair under the window.

She looks around her, sighs with pleasure and says: I will stay in bed today.

What a surprise! In the hospital she insisted on sitting up every day. So I help her into her white nightie with rosebuds printed on it, and into bed.

I sit outside her window and smoke. I feel as if I am resurfacing from a mud pile. The relief of having her comfortable is enormous.

The garden round the house is so beautiful. The wild

bank at the back is lush with ferns and there are a few
mauve cyclamen hiding under the growing wild
strawberries. The azaleas are still red but fading.
The foxgloves are coming, and so are the dandelions —
everywhere! I must ask Tony to come with his 'lads' to
clear up the rough stuff. He cares for the gardens in
our community with a team of extraordinary characters,
wonderful people with special needs. The daffodils are
finished but not yet ready for the leaves to be pulled.
The sides and front of the house are bare, now without
the yellow of the daffs, and the periwinkles are blue
bits of sky on the ground. I need more garden plants to
give less space to the weeds.

I am thankful to nature. It is not as bright as the
garden on the other side, its colours more coarse, but
its beauty is endless, nevertheless. I want to take
Mother out, for a last walk, but she cannot today, she
is too tired.

Now the family arrive: Agnes and Christine, her
youngest daughter, and also two of Liz's children,
Ruthie and Matthew.

We talk about the last unction. Mother wants the whole
family to be present. She gets so excited she starts to
list off all her friends too! In the end I am brutal (as
usual) and I ask her who this ritual is for, herself or
the whole world and is it a PR exercise or a serious
business? She says: Veronika, you are so hard! But then
she agrees that the family and two other friends, who are
our neighbours, are really all she wants present.

The priest is the husband of the nurse, and also an old
friend. How lucky we are to have so many kind and useful

friends around us! He explains how the last unction releases one from one's ties on earth and one can go freely to the other side. He says we should not be surprised if she lets go very soon after the event.

All the people from the community visit her. Now that she is home it is so easy just to pop in. She loves to see them, beaming at everyone, but cannot manage long, serious visits. I ration those still.

Bedtime is once more fun. She has her own bathroom again! How pleased she is, and how grateful. She doesn't ask for a bedtime story but commands me: Take out the flowers. A good nurse never leaves them in the sickroom overnight! She is truly back to her old self, but in flashes, fading out at other times. Her spirit is as bright as ever, her body almost gone. I can lift her with ease.

18 May

It is Saturday again and the small group meets to read to the nature beings outside her window. Mother shows no interest, she is far away, confused after the night. The Piriton, which she takes before sleeping, has again left her vacant.

As we are all together now, we make the big decision and I call the undertaker. He comes with the priest, and as Mother dozes in her room we sit in the kitchen and cheerfully plan her funeral.

George, the undertaker, is wonderful. He is pragmatic and yet kind, telling us all the ways we can celebrate her death. In the end we decide on a plain unvarnished coffin with a cream cotton lining, no embalming. We will lay her out ourselves, with Eva's help, and she will be taken to the chapel for the three

nights' wake. This is what she wants. And she will wear
her white Sunday dress. She asked me this a long time
ago. This makes us all laugh, she is as ever vain,
because that dress is very elegant with a hand-made
lace collar and suits her beautifully. With her so-
yellow skin now, she will look gorgeous!

The phone rings all day, friends come to see her, we
offer tea and cake. It is like a party. I cook and cook,
and tell Mother what fun we are having. She sits
enthroned in her chair in her beautiful room and holds
court to one after another, loving it all. And we visit
too, to refresh ourselves in the well of peace that
surrounds her. Though so shrunken in body, her
grandeur is as a queen's.

I am privileged to be the person she asks to help her
with her physical care — she demands only me. She says
we have worked ourselves into a comfortable team. Each
knows what the other plans next and so the movements are
smooth and gentle to her tender skin and bones.

Midnight, I hear her groaning beneath me. I run down.
She is restless, neither awake nor asleep, telling
someone to go away, groaning and sighing. I sit with her
till she is calm. She does not really wake up at all.

In the darkness, I wonder about the pain of getting
out of one's body. That shining pillar of light has to
shed the body like a grub its cocoon. I say the Lord's
Prayer for her and she is peaceful again.

19-May

Sunday breakfast, Liz feeds Mother, who takes a bit of
porridge. We realize we have forgotten the weekly
Saturday night Bible reading. Even in the hospital I
remembered! Now we are so happy to be together, we

Three sisters. Left to right: me, Mother, Agnes and Liz

forget all traditions! Even Mother forgot. So we tell
her, she laughs a little and says: Let's do it now. I
cannot go to the service anyway.

We sit round her chair, the three daughters with
their mother. I feel a lump of happiness in my throat.
It is Whit Sunday and we read the traditional Acts 2:
1-12, about the disciples and the tongues of flame
descending.

Mother begins a conversation, as is tradition. She is
completely awake, alight with joy. She talks about how
people receive spiritual deeds here on earth. Some
will perceive the spirit as a flame on the heads of
those who act from the spirit. Others will only see
madness, idiocy or black magic. It depends on one's own
inner striving what one will see. The young of today see
so much more clearly than did her generation, they are
not so materialistic. She says they see into one's
innermost soul, and make their judgements of another
human being based on better insight than people of her
generation did. We talk about the Manichaeans, those
people who believe that it is not correct to slay evil,
as one did in the old days, but to enter into the evil and
find the good that lies within, and so overcome the
darkness. Through darkness one can find the light. In
dying, new life can be born.

Mother sits in her chair, wearing her other Sunday
dress, dove-grey and beautiful, made from the finest
spun wool. She is enthroned in her chair, golden and
serene, and completely with us.

Quietly, she waits for the afternoon and for the
priest with the last unction. During her rest after a
lunch she has taken in a cup, I sit and smoke again. I
see, above the grey stone wall, under the sandthorn

tree, a glimpse of red. It is the first rose, deep and
slightly open, scented as richly as only the red rose
can be. I pick it and put it in a glass vase beside my
mother's chair where she sits ready for the priest. But
before his arrival, she is visited by Christof, maybe
her oldest friend, though much younger than her, whom
she looked after when he was a child. She still has a
fondness for him that we three daughters sometimes
thought to be greater than her love for us. She is
deeply and radiantly happy to talk to him. But half an
hour is all she can manage.

At 5.00 p.m. the priest arrives. We stand in a circle
squashed into her room. She sits, her eyes fixed
painfully on him, a very tall thin man, and listens with
her whole being to his words, watching every movement
he makes. As a young man he had known her, and she was a
kind of mentor to him. Now he stands straight and reads
the words. While reading and anointing tears fall onto
his book, though his powerful words never falter. We
are all greatly moved with the power of the spirit. I
see light everywhere, blinding and yet healing. The
grandchildren sob quietly, smiles on their faces.

   Afterwards, when the priest has left the room to
change out of his vestments, my mother says strongly:
Thank you all, all you dear people.

   A tear falls from each eye, as though on cue and she
smiles. Agnes embraces her and whispers something,
then Liz, then the others do the same, one by one.

   I cannot hear what they say, I am half here, half on
the other side seeing the bright white pillar of light
that envelops my small upright mother.

   They have all gone to the kitchen, I kiss my mother.

She says: Veronika, make the priest some tea! He will be thirsty.

I go out laughing. She is still boss in her own home.

Today the weather has been muted, silent and a bit sultry, though not warm. During the last unction the wind got up, roaring with power around the house. As soon as the priest had spoken the last word, the rain fell down as though from a bucket, lashing the windows. The clouds were dark and heavy.

Now the evening sun, brilliant and red, is glowing hot over the lough. It is 9.00 p.m. The sun has just sunk behind the hills and I sit smoking, whilst a robin in the wild cherry tree is singing its heart out, all by itself, as though crazy with joy. Nature is saluting my mother! I am enchanted and run in to get my sisters. When they come out, the robin has gone, and dusk has spread its wings over the earth. There is only the remnants of a red sunset over the lough. Was I here, or there? The two sides of life are very intertwined right now.

20 May

A quiet night. Everyone slept. I did not hear my mother. We three sisters, Agnes, Liz, Veronika, are all in one room, just like kids! We chatted till late, laughing and enjoying ourselves. Three middle-aged children!

It's rainy and windy, a miserable blusterous day. We talk about the nature spirits that Mother gave so much thought to. They are here in the wind and the rain.

Eva tells us that Mother hardly managed the few steps to the bathroom. She is completely exhausted after her wash and lies prostrate in her bed, looking weepy. So now we will keep all care to the bedroom.

No, says our strong-willed mother, not the toilet. I
will not have a potty-chair! So we wheel her to the
toilet today. What a palaver! No eating either, today.
A few sips of water is all she will take, even with Liz's
gentle handling.

I have the pleasant task of phoning the consultant to
tell him she will not be returning to the hospital. He
tries to persuade me she will get better care there! We
have a bizarre conversation in which I diagnose that
she is dying of cancer of the pancreas, and he agrees!
But then he admits: It is really very difficult to say
how long someone will take to die of an illness.
Everyone goes in their own time. Usually I cannot tell
relatives that their parent is dying. They don't want
to hear. But I see you are quite able to take the truth.

I thank him for his honesty. He says: No, I should
thank you. You have made my job so much easier. Please
give my respects to Mrs Lipsker.

I am deeply impressed. What a terrible thing it is to
have to tell lies at someone's death-bed, at the very
moment when the truth is paramount.

I bring Mother the good news that she will not have to
return to the hospital. She responds tepidly. She sits
in her chair and broods. She seems less and less
interested in what goes on outside her room. She sleeps
in her chair. She is completely at peace, and not the
least depressed any more, simply remote and quiet.

The rest of our large family phone in one after the
other. It seems that by Thursday we will all be
together, children, husbands and grandchildren, not
to mention the great-grandchildren.

Frédérique, my dearest friend and sister-in-law,

could not make it for the last unction. My tactless reaction to her help in the hospital has not yet been forgiven. I cannot find the energy to repair the damage. I think I must give it all to my mother. Afterwards, I will take up the challenge of healing the hurts I have done and am doing. Now is not the time. Now my sister-in-law will be away for a week. It is likely Mother will not be here when she comes back, but we have to accept that Frédérique has other commitments to honour. Agnes, too, has to go back to Holland. We agree we will call her before it is too late — flights are cheap and readily available.

So for a few hours, there is only us again — Rob, me, Mother, Rachel, Tony and Elizabeth, plus my sister Liz. The others go their separate ways.

Mother doesn't want Rachel to bring the little one — she says it is not fitting for Elizabeth to be with a dying person. We disagree. Elizabeth has barely come to earth, just about a year ago. She still remembers the other side. So she visits. How strangely she behaves, as though Mother were not here at all! She treats her like a ghost, playing at her feet but seeing her somewhere else.

Rebekah, Max and Alexandra arrive. Rebekah is Liz's youngest daughter. Alexandra is the newest great-grandchild. Mother holds her and croons, enjoying the freshness of new life. But she tires quickly and asks them to go. She will see them tomorrow.

21 May

No more walking even across the room from bed to chair. The indoor wheelchair is paying off. I see Mother can

hardly even sit in her chair, but she will not go to bed.
No food, but she drinks sips of water.

Today she said good-bye to Elizabeth. She held her on
her knee and said sternly: Good-bye, liebchen
(darling). Rachel took her out and wept.

We have new life outside. The garden has done with
spring and needs a clean-up for summer. Tony has come
with the estate team, a group of noisy individuals, all
severely disabled, and they begin to clear, cut, tidy
and edge. The sounds of human beings, sometimes
peculiar noises because so many are disabled, rings
around the house. Mother sits in her chair and hears
them. She is grateful because she loves the garden. I
sit quietly with her and think of all the hundreds of
children she has helped in her life's work dedicated to
people with disabilities. I think it fitting they
should now want to do something for her.

Agnes has left for Holland, with Christine. I seem to
move from quiet concern for Mother to wild bed-making
and room-cleaning. I love sitting with Mother. It
fills me with strength.

Two great friends of Mother have arrived from South
Africa, Peter and Susanne. Mother is filled with
happiness. They sit with her, talking. We do not
interfere or censor their visits. They, and Christof,
are privileged friends from far back and she needs
their love. Erika visits too, but has to go again.
Mother is occupied with her friends and Erika feels she
should not interfere. I find this difficult, as she
gave so many years to Mother, but she insists that
Mother needs them more than her, at this time.

Life is a bit like a hotel. We have guests all the
time. I make tea, coffee, meals, clean, cut fresh

flowers, and wish the days of Mother and me alone (those
days I so resented!) were back. Oh, well, the grass is
always greener . . . and all that!

She still wants me to see her to bed. I love those
times. We chat, and I kneel at her feet to take off her
shoes. As always she says, Thank you, Veronika.

I am very tired and a little frightened too.

22 May

The night was only slightly disturbed by groaning. I
was so tired I couldn't get up, so I lay waiting to see if
she would settle, which she did. But now I feel guilty
because she was so alone with her pain and maybe fears.

She looks like a gold and silver queen, I tell her. She
is flattered and smiles. How charming she is today,
full of vitality. She asks me to check her knitting. I
correct the mistakes and she takes it in her hands and
tries to knit. She cannot do it any more. The skill has
left her. She laughs gaily and says: I will knit one row
and then put it away.

I help her with every stitch, seeing how her fingers
will no longer obey her strong will. She puts down the
bright red scarf she had been knitting for the great-
grandson and says: No more.

After her lunch rest she decides she will not get up
any more. She says tiredly: I have not got the strength.
So we discuss the toilet visits and decide on nappies
from now on. I sit with her, but she does not want
anything except my company. Suddenly she sits bolt
upright and says: Du luegst! (You are lying!) Her
German sounds terrible and harsh. Then she begins to
groan and moan and turn restlessly, scratching

herself. She is mumbling unintelligibly, and seems quite demented.

We take turns to sit with her. We will not leave her alone any more. My guilt of the night floods back and I feel awful.

She is sore wherever one touches her, her back, her legs, her heels, her arms. She groans with pain all over.

Visitors come in streams. We announce each one of them and ask her whether she want to see them. She sees each one, pulling herself together to be gracious and dignified. We sit in the kitchen and want to weep for her tremendous self-discipline that will not allow her to give in to her misery.

In between the visits she complains of flies, that they buzz round her. So we get the fly-swatter and go on hunts, giggling like idiots. She lies sunken in her dying flesh and scratches wantonly.

Her doctor visits. I sit outside whilst she is there, smoking in the quiet air of early summer. The garden is looking good — cleared, but not quite finished. The team will still need to finish edging the flower-beds.

The doctor says it is now a matter of days. We know this, but now we have to be practical. I phone the undertaker. George says he has the perfect coffin and has found some cotton lining, unusual because they only use nylon. He found a bit in a cupboard somewhere, left over from long ago! I tell him he is wonderful. He says everything is now ready.

I ring Agnes, she will come tomorrow. Liz and I want us all to be together for the event of her going and we hope she will hang on till Agnes comes.

A storm blows up. All hell is blasting round the house. The struggle inside Mother is raging outside too. But the evening is radiant, lucid and clear, washed clean by the wind and rain. I sit on my seat in the garden and see a white butterfly resting on the one red rose that came after I picked the first one for my mother. The white creature sits and preens its feathered wings, readying them for flight. The breeze is soft and singing through the sandthorn tree. There is a reverent hush after the wildness of the storm.

This night Mother groans and calls endlessly. She cannot sleep, is tortured by flies, cries out that she is in a pit, please to get her out. She rolls about. I cannot leave her. I do not want to call Liz, who has sat with her so long during the day, so I begin to sing her lullabies, songs she sang to us as children. She grows gradually more peaceful, holds my hand and sighs.

When the 'flies' come again, as they do in spells, I light candles, turning off the electric light, and say the Lord's Prayer. She is, once more, comforted. The next attack, I stroke her head, gently, as she did for me when I was a child and ill in bed. She lies quietly for a while, then pushes my hand impatiently away and says, pettishly: You can stop combing me now, I am quite beautiful enough!

I get a terrible fit of the giggles, which ends in tears. Then I read to her from St John's Gospel, the verses at the beginning that she used to love. Finally she goes to sleep. It is five in the morning.

23 May

The GP visits. He sits with her quietly, because she appears to be asleep. Suddenly, she wakes, sits up, opens her eyes and says: Thank you, dear Doctor. Now I must say good-bye.

She offers him her hand and shakes his warmly. He comes out with me to the sitting room, looking stunned.

Your mother is a very powerful lady, he says. I agree that she is indeed wonderful, but is very afraid of pain. I tell him I have promised not to let her suffer too much. He says that if she needs them, I can give her painkillers, but it is not a good idea unless she is really in great distress. Her liver, he says, will not cope with them.

We decide it is time to institute night duty and make a rota between the three of us. Agnes, having sorted out her business at home in Holland, will be back here by tonight. So we start with me, Liz will do Friday, Agnes can take Saturday and so on. This gives each of us a day off after night duty. I look forward to tomorrow!

We contact the district nurse for bed supports and other aids.

Then the visitors start up again!

The priest comes for coffee, and to give Mother Communion. I tell her he is here and she sits up, hair awry, groans tormentedly and calls: Yes, please come and give me the last onion!

I rush out giggling hysterically, because as she speaks, the priest enters in his vestments! I cry with laughter, unable to tell the others.

People phone to arrange visiting times. All are reasonable except one, who says he will come Saturday. I try to tell him she may not be able to see him by then as she is fading fast. He is very angry, tells me I cannot prevent him, I get distressed. In the end, we agree that

we cannot prevent any visits until she says herself
that she has had enough. Communion has strengthened
her. She lies peacefully, occasionally scratching,
and seems to sleep a bit.

I leave her for a moment, Liz is resting, I hear Mother
call. As I come in she says in agony: I am so full of sin!

I hold her hand and she sinks into sleep again.

Things are moving very, very fast now. Liz and I go
outside to my bench so that I can smoke but where we can
still hear Mother, and so that we can take stock. We
need more than a rota now. We need all the practical
help we can get so that we three daughters can have
quality time with our mother. She cannot be left alone
at all, because even her sleep is troubled, infested
with flies, black pits, nightmares of being trapped.
Is this what it feels like to be stuck in a decomposing
physical body, like a black fly-pit?

We talk about my seeing Mother at the river enveloped
in a pillar of white light. This is surely the spiritual
truth, but the other truth of rotting bodies as prisons
of the soul is also real.

The practical implications include the necessity to
move Mother's bed, as it stands in the corner and must
now be free standing to enable assistance from either
side. I know Mother will hate this. Her nightmares are
ones of insecurity, of Nazi soldiers, of falling, of
intruders who touch her head, visitors whom she
identifies as a boy and a girl who stand by her bed and
want something, wordlessly yearning, and she does not
understand them. They leave her when she turns her face
to the wall. Moving her bed will be dreadfully
traumatic. But it must be done.

We will ask the family, our sons-in-law and daughters

who have arrived one by one, to take over cleaning and catering. The night rota is already fixed.

Mother groans and Liz leaves me. I sit on alone, struggling with my drifting awareness of the two worlds that are in reality one. The garden here is ready for the summer, the 'lads' will soon be here, it is nearly work-time. But now it is peaceful, small birds twittering, the roses about to burst into bloom.

The clouds drift slowly and the light changes from earthly sun to bright moments of the other light. Colours deepen and fade, I am neither here nor there. Mother stands at the narrow river, gazing intently into the water, black and still as a volcanic lake.

We lift Mother, in her bed, placing the head end at the wall, the feet towards the window. Now it is free standing. She is extremely angry, though we have explained its necessity very thoroughly.

She is disorientated on top of everything else. I want to cry, as I feel her anger and frustration at our removing the last bit of her free will. She demands to be taken to the toilet, but cannot rise. Her back hurts her terribly. Every time I touch her, she gasps with pain. She thrashes about in her bed as though fighting someone or something. Her expression is ugly, sunken and old. Her yellow golden skin looks sallow. For the first time I see that she is ancient, a crone of nine hundred years, an oracle about to deliver curses. I want to embrace her, soothe her, bring back the mother whose wisdom has guided so many on their life's path.

The flies torment her. They come in through the open crack of the window, necessary to expel the odour of dying, and crawl on her white sheets, black as hell. We

draw the white curtains as a screen to keep out the
little devils, and protect her from the eyes of the
garden team. She is restless and grim, even in sleep.

I sit by her bed, stroke her hand and tell her about
the garden. I talk about the one round our house, but
really it is about the garden of light. It all gets
mixed up. She grows a bit calmer. Why do I not come right
out and tell her where she is? I cannot. She has never
liked my visions, saying I should not believe I may be
given such gifts. She has always been very much my
mother, even while respecting the fact that we have,
for most of my adult years, been colleagues. So I keep
silent about the pillar of white light.

Tonight we are all three together to settle our
mother. We choose the lullabies as they come to our
memory, smiling, reverting to childhood, soothing our
mother, as she soothed us. Impulsively, we say our
childrens' prayer, instead of the Lord's Prayer,
without needing to prime each other. We simply begin:

Thou angel of God
Who has charge of me
From the dear father
Of mercifulness.
Thou shepherding kind
Of the fold of the saints
To keep watch round about me
This night.
Be thou a bright flame before me
Be thou a guiding star above me
Be thou a smooth path below me
And be a kindly shepherd behind me

Today, tonight, and for ever.
I am tired and I am a stranger
Lead thou me to the land of angels.
For me it is time to go home
To the court of Christ
To the peace of Heaven.

Amen.

She lies still, a little grim smile on her lips, in the flickering candle-light. We leave her, my sisters to go to bed in my room, silent and wakeful. I am on duty for this night.

It is dramatic! Mother spends most of the night calling, groaning: Put me back in the corner! Pull me out, the pit is drowning me, the flies, oh, the ghastly flies!

She tries to get out of bed. I sit at her side and hold her hand and leg gently, keeping her from falling out, singing lullabies in the candle-light. Liz appears soundlessly, sits on the other side and sings softly with me. Mother quietens for a bit, then the fight starts again. I fetch the Bible and read from St John's Gospel. She seems to listen, groaning softly now, but we can see that the agony is building.

Then she really shouts, the pain is great. I remember my promise not to let her suffer pain too long. We decide that now she needs the painkillers. Will they kill her? We give her two. Eventually she sighs and groans: They do nothing for the pain, the pit, oh the pit! She starts to plead for Rob to come and pull her out. She commands us: He must take me by the head and pull really hard. Pull my ego out! Now! Fetch Rob!

Her faith in him is touching. He has always fixed

things for her and she so admired his handyman skills.
She always said to me that he was a good man with great
spiritual potential. She used to say he had a loving
nature. Now she holds to this faith and expects him to
pull out her essential being, free her from her body for
the other side! Our impotence makes me weep.

You will have to do it yourself, I say cruelly. This is
your task. We will stay with you until it is done.

Liz strokes her gently, whispering songs, then we
stop singing and recite the Lord's Prayer as the sun
makes its presence known by lifting the darkness in a
grey pre-dawn light. She sleeps, at last, exhausted
from the battle.

24 May

5.00 a.m.
We sit in the kitchen, make coffee, exhausted, and
talk. What a comfort to be together. Agnes sleeps on,
while Liz and I chat.

Mother is finding it so hard to get out of her body.
The trap is set so tight, she cannot leave. We talk
about the other side. If she can see the light, which we
believe she can, then why must she struggle so hard? Why
does the body hold on so tightly? Is this what she means
when she says she has told so many lies? Is this why she
exclaimed so challengingly to someone, or something,
Du luegst! which means: 'You are lying'? Isn't life in
the body a lie, compared to the wholeness of life on the
other side? Here we only experience in time — we see
things one after the other, the events taking on an
appearance of a stream, or river of life. But there we
know it all together — all lives as one space. We are one

with the ocean of light beings, a single drop melded
into one vast sea.

What a relief death must be, but how frightening to
exchange time-consciousness with one of space.

The trap she talks about, wails to be pulled out of, is
a wicked one — and yet it contains also the good deeds,
not only the bad. But letting go of it cannot be easy
because 'it' holds onto you, rather than you holding on
to it. This is the Big Lie.

We talk about keeping people alive. It must be the
ultimate agony of soul to be kept alive in the body when
the body is no longer viable to your consciousness — a
living hell.

7.30 a.m.

Eva comes. She gives a bed-bath. I help her as the care
of the body is my task, Liz seeing to the food. Agnes,
now awake and in the kitchen with us, agrees to take on
booking in the visitors. I cannot cope with their
demands on Mother. It tires her so, calls her back to
life here when she wants to be left in peace to take her
last journey. But we hold true to what we decided with
the priest. It is not our decision to censor the guests.
She will either say when she has had enough or will go
out into another state of consciousness. Agnes says
she can manage the stream of visits and space them out,
making sure Mother knows who wants to see her, and that
she can be given the opportunity to say whether she
wants to see them.

While being bathed Mother looks like a tiny yellow
wax doll, the sort you stick pins into. She shivers and
moans with every move, unable today to say her
customary Thank you.

I ask for the day off. I cannot cope any more. I need time to myself, time to grieve, perhaps, although I am not sad.

Liz and Agnes take on the day-care. I will be around in the evening again.

10.00 a.m.

I have had an urge to work in the garden. I go out to the garden centre and buy beautiful flowering plants in a sort of mad delight. I will make the garden round the house a poor reflection of the other side, reds, golds, blues, purples and various shades of green. I spend a great deal of money!

Meanwhile, the grandchildren take care of their babies and clean, cook, make coffee and are simply wonderful. I come home to a lovely house, smiling people and a great sense of peace. I wander round the garden, which has been cleared and prepared by Tony and the garden team, and place the new plants where I think they will flourish. From inside, the others encourage me through the windows, waving and agreeing with my decisions. We will have a garden like no other this summer. And Mother will be in a garden like no other. What is beyond the light? Where do the dead go once they have recognized the beings and have been made welcome? What is the dark shadow in the distance to one side of the river? I don't want to think about it — it doesn't seem very welcoming and fills me with not a little apprehension.

2.30 p.m.

I sit outside on the bench and smoke. I listen to Mother's heart-rending groans, and I do not go to her.

It is torture! I know my sisters are with her, it is my day off, I need the space, but I am tortured nevertheless. But I sit and smoke and gaze at the garden and make plans for its beauty.

Susanne and Peter are still here. They come and spend hours sitting with Mother, quietly and supportively, whilst she groans and struggles.

Poor Erika! Whenever she has visited today, they are there, and she goes again, humbly giving them the time to be with her dear friend because they have travelled from so far to see her.

4.00p.m.
Christof comes with his wife. They do not stay long and I hear through the window (open for the fresh air) how Mother says firmly as though dismissing them: Good-bye. Be well.

They leave, tears falling silently, quite unashamed of their emotion. Christof says nothing, walking quickly away.

Others visit, and they too stay very briefly. They leave as though chastened — not in a negative way, but as though challenged to 'do the good'.

Mother is calling for me. I run to her, and she says piteously: My back is so painful. Please, allow me to die. Angel of Death, come and take me!

Then she says: Veronika, what must I do to be allowed to die?

I say sadly: You have to be patient. The angel will take you into his arms when the time is right. We all have the right time to go, so you have to wait and accept.

She is comforted by such straight talking and seems relieved. She sleeps a little.

5.00 p.m.
The flies torment her again, though now we cannot see them. We have killed every one of the devils, but the unseen creatures come in hosts. Her battle with earthly death has begun. She writhes and shouts and scratches, making ugly faces and mumbling in a demented way.

She eats nothing, nor passes anything all day. Now she says suddenly, quite lucidly and firmly: No more visitors. I cannot cope with their needs any more.

When I tell the others, there is a sigh of relief. Now we can say 'no' to everyone. How will the man who comes tomorrow take it when he cannot see her? I worry about that. He is a close friend of hers, and under other circumstances she would have wanted to see him. The others say: Don't worry, he will accept it. I know he won't, he is a very determined person. I worry about him. Will he think I engineered this? They say: If you know you didn't, it doesn't matter what he thinks. Stop being so selfish. Think of Mother! They are all quite cross with me.

The house is so still. There is an air of expectancy, like before a birthday, when as a child you lie wakeful in your bed, waiting for the candle to bring its birthday light into the dark room. We talk in whispers, move slowly, and sit quietly together over supper.

7.00 p.m.
Mother is bruised all over her body! How did the marks get there? As we gently wash her, we see that each tiny pressure by our soft hands leaves a blue mark!

Agnes asks Mother for her teeth. Through all these days and nights she has kept them in her mouth, her vanity now an endearing quality that affords her dignity and upholds her sinking spirits. To our amazement, she opens her mouth and tongues them out. Her hearing-aid she has taken out this afternoon by herself, after declaring she would see no more visitors.

We make her comfortable, looking forward to settling her with songs and prayers. We three sisters now communicate without much speaking — we are entirely in tune with each other. We sit by her bedside and delight in her warmth. She emanates an air as of a baby, cosy in its crib. The fight seems to be over, she lies peacefully, warm in her white bridal bed, Death, her bridegroom, is very near to her at last.

The day has been rainy, windy, with sunny interludes, and rather cold. I am the only one who has been outside. Rob is home from work and suggests we three women go out for a walk. He will sit with Mother. He has hardly seen her, only listened to my accounts and been a hugely cheerful support. We see he wants to take his leave of his mother-in-law. As soon as he is seated and I am about to go, she sits up, snatches his hand and, like a witch, stages a death-bed scene Victorians would have been so proud of! She begs him never to leave me, and demands of me to honour my dear husband. Stay together, she whines, pathetically, Promise me you will never part.

I am sorry to say, but in the face of this look-alike apparition of my sensible mother, I behave appallingly. I laugh hysterically, not able to take her seriously. Rob is wonderfully calm and serious, soothing her and making all the promises she wants.

What a woman! I won't make any promises in such a manipulative moment!

My sisters laugh till the tears come over this scene, but mercifully in the kitchen and not at her bedside as I did. She always did say I was a naughty girl and had no reverence!

8.30 p.m.

As we walk across the estate towards the chapel, intent on picking out and marking the spot for her urn to be buried in, the air is calm and fresh. The hushed peace of the house has spread all over the gardens and paths and woods and rocks. The bluebells under the trees along the way are like a carpet, thick and dark, waving slightly in the little gusts of warm May wind.

The moon rises, golden, like a full new penny. We walk home, hardly speaking, only to agree that she will cross over tonight. As babies are born at the full or new moon, so do we know the old choose this door too. We are very happy.

When we get home the grandchildren, who are staying in a neighbour's house, telephone to say that whilst we were out they saw a rainbow over the house, and now, from their window, the moonlight has silvered the roof tiles.

We go out and we see a silvery shimmer over everything, the garden radiating with moving, living colour in the darkness of the night. And the robin, all alone, is singing his heart out again. Now my sisters see it too, and hear the singular birdsong.

9.30 p.m.

It is time to settle her. We sing one lullaby after the other, and she lies quietly, listening intently. All of a sudden, in the warmth of the candle-light, we run out of songs and stare at each other. Then we begin 'The Christ Child's Lullabye' together, without speaking about it first.

> My joy, my love, my darling thou,
> My treasure new, my rapture thou,
> My comely beauteous babe-son thou,
> Unworthy I to tend to thee.

Chorus:

> Alleluia

> White sun of hope and light art thou,
> Of love the heart and I art thou,
> Though but a tender babe, I bow
> In heavenly rapture unto thee.

Chorus:

> Alleluia

Mother opens her shrunken cracked dry lips and sings with us:

> Alleluia.

She quavers in perfect tune, keeping time and staring with her nearly blind blue eyes into the candlelit darkness.

I cannot sing, I break up completely, sobbing softly. My mother was comforter, challenger, chastiser, friend, confidante, spur and shield for me all my life. Now she will be gone and she gives us her Alleluia in praise of life and death. My sisters hug me, comforting my rare tears. They too are moved.

Mother groans again, into the wonder of that moment, begging the Angel of Death again: Come now!

She pleads: I am ready, take me now!

She says: Veronika, what must I do? Her voice carries full confidence in me, that I will know the answer.

Then she says: Lieselienchen, mein Herz, you really must go to bed. Her voice for my sister carries all the weight of loving concern.

Then she says: Agnes, you are my good daughter! Her voice carries all the satisfaction of a job well done.

Now I cry again, this time in farewell. This is the death moment of parting that is truly worthy of my mother's lifelong commitment to truth.

11.00p.m.

I sleep in another room, where I cannot hear my mother. It is the first time since weeks that I can sleep peacefully, because my sisters will listen out for her. It is Liz's turn to sit with her.

Mother is very restless, tossing, moving, reaching out, waving her arm in the air, reaching up, up, up.

Now she speaks in German, her mother tongue: Wahres Spiegelbild (True mirror-image).

After some more quiet agony of time: Esoterischer Schüler (Esoteric pupil).

Time passes, she is restless and reaching for something. She says: Die Tür steht auf (The door is open).

Then, quite soon after that statement: Die gute Geister (The good spirits).

After many hours during which these statements are uttered at intervals, she says powerfully: Die Sinnen bewahren! (Retain the senses!)

Liz is quiet throughout, only stroking her and humming softly, trying to bring Mother's arms under the duvet because she is so cold. The night is very long. Mother's struggle to move into the light seems endless to my sister, but she is intensely grateful to be able to follow her journey by the short announcements she makes.

25 May

Mother lies peacefully after her last words, announcing that she will retain her senses. Liz is exhausted. She cannot stay with her any more. She goes upstairs to her bed and falls instantly into a deep sleep. She dreams that she sees Mother sitting in her chair in the kitchen, quite well and beaming, wearing a blue dress with tiny white roses printed on it and trimmed with a lace collar. People are there with her, having tea and chatting. Behind her someone has delivered a wooden crate and people are unpacking it, making a huge mess with sawdust and paper bits of packaging. Liz is greatly distressed. Can't they see that Mother is dying and they shouldn't be making such a mess and commotion? She is suddenly wide awake and runs downstairs to Mother.

Agnes had noticed her coming to bed and says of this event: Liz lay down for a maximum of five minutes!

Mother's breathing has changed. Agnes can hear it from her bed in the room above, so she gets up and joins Liz.

6.00 a.m.

Mother is breathing hard and deliberately, every breath drawn in and driven out like a bellows.

Her hard breath goes on and on. My sisters sit by her stroking her hands for comfort and also for encouragement.

6.30 a.m.

Liz calls me. I sit with my sisters, we hold Mother's hands and gently stroke them. The dawn is coming, faintly lighting up the sky outside her room.

Mother's breathing slows and she begins to sound like a mechanical pump. In . . . out . . . in . . . out . . . in . . . out . . .

I fetch Rob. He comes down and sits at the foot of her bed, silently watching, keeping watch over us all. We start to sing 'The Christ Child's Lullabye', instinctively knowing this is the best of all songs for her. We are filled with the strength of joy, of expectancy of the gathering moment.

Mother labours strongly, as though in childbirth, her expression intent. She looks like a shrivelled yellow apelet, and enormous love wells up in us, pouring out towards her, embracing her efforts to release the brightness of her being from the waxy corpse of her body.

She shivers, uncontrollable, hands slack in our grasp.

Agnes says: She is gone.

We know she has made it, made the crossing at last, though her body goes on breathing laboriously.

The rhythm changes to a light, slow tempo, she opens her eyes, gazing up and outwards, then she squeezes them shut, cramps her limbs and gives a mighty push, delivering her spirit.

7.15 a.m.

She breathes out on a long, steady breath, her eyes wide open. Then she closes them, and a smile of pure gentleness rests on her lips. She is at peace.

We sit quietly and let go her hands, at peace at last.

We stand up, all four of us, and smile in gratitude. Our mother has triumphed over the clinging of her body and is victoriously free.

7.30 a.m.

We have had our moment of peace. Now the reality starts. I phone the doctor.

Eva arrives and we begin to organize the laying out. I don't want to help. My job was to care for the living and dying body. My sisters can care for the corpse.

The priest arrives and the undertaker. Business as usual. But not quite. We ask George if he would like to see her. He looks at her, smiles and gently strokes her head. He says: She was a great lady.

8.30 a.m.

I get Helen Barbara up. She stands next to her grandmother, serious and pale in her nightie. She knows about death and is quiet. Her love for her grandmother is palpable, though she cannot say it in words.

The doctors come to write out the death certificate. They are very kind, though I am still in my nightie!

Erika and her friend come, they stay a moment with Mother, then go to read to the nature spirits. It is, after all Saturday, and Mother kept to her daily rhythms most strictly! They read for her too, honouring her self-discipline and warm unsentimentality.

I notice that the weather is dull and soft, a grey cloud-cover over all. It is remarkably silent — even the tractors are not working today. I smoke in peace on the bench under her window. Then I go in and start to phone friends and family who cannot be here with us.

11.00 a.m.

I want to sit outside, on my bench, smoke and be with nature, the weather, the birds and the garden on the other side — but the phone keeps ringing and ringing. In between, I try to reach all those people I know will want to hear the good news, and of course they want all the details. My voice is hoarse. I feel as high as a kite, jubilant and exhausted. My sisters ring their own contacts, their faces look the way mine feels, pink-cheeked, flushed, radiant smiles and serious, grave moments. We are truly elated from emotion and tiredness.

The weather is lovely, springlike, with even some early summer warmth. The birds sing like mad, busy caring for their nestlings. They come to feed off the kitchen windowsill where we put out sunflower seeds for them.

In Mother's room, my sisters and Eva wash her little shrivelled body and lay her out in her white Sunday dress. Agnes puts her teeth back in. Mother would have so disliked being seen without them! Agnes feels that we should honour her vanity to the last, since it was this very quality that helped her to leave her body so graciously. We gather afterwards and lay single white roses and mauve friesias on her, Helen Barbara taking charge and arranging them in a pattern. Mother lies peacefully, golden and silver beneath her flowers, smiling gently.

Tony arrives, thrusting a bunch of yellow rosebuds into my hand. I thank him and say that Mother would love them. No, he says, these are not for the dead, but for the living. I am moved to tears.

Lunch is bread and cheese, together, all eleven or so of us. The whole family seems to be here, and yet I know some are still to come. I have lost count. People come and go. Susanne and Peter have gone out to make a flower bunch for the coffin when it will be moved to the chapel.

2.15 p.m.

Friends and neighbours gather in the chapel to read a verse for Mother. Agnes goes on our behalf and tells of her last moments.

I stay at home, alone at last, on the bench in the garden. But I cannot cross over. I want to, so very badly. I want to see the light receiving the bright shining pillar that is my mother now. But there is a wall between us. The way is barred.

I know I must observe precisely all the things that will now follow on this side of the river. They will be echoes of the joy of the light on the other side. Both sides are one, here and there.

3.00 p.m.

George comes with another man and the coffin. It is plain unvarnished pine, a simple box with a natural linen lining. They lift Mother gently from the bed, flowers and all, and rest her comfortably in the coffin. They take it in the hearse to the chapel and place it on wooden stands. We put tall candles at her head.

And the flowers start coming!

A wild bouquet, delicately picked by Susanne lies at her feet. All around her, the abundance of colour grows. In between are small vases of bluebells, wood anemones and celandines, patches of wild cow parsley (dreadful for the hay-fever sufferers, who sneeze when they come to see her!). The great-grandchildren have brought them from walks in the woods.

Huib (Agnes's husband), Theo (the partner of Andrea who is Agnes's eldest daughter), Ruthie (Liz's eldest daughter) and Christine (Agnes's youngest daughter) arrive. Andrea and Hadewych (Agnes's next daughter, with her partner Corneel) have been here all week. They are the grandchildren who saw the rainbow.

We arrange the wake. Someone will always be with Mother between 10.00 p.m. and 6.00 a.m. for the next three nights. We book family time for the first two hours of each evening.

Visitors from all over the world start to come. Neighbours and friends organize their beds and transports. I am so glad of their help, glad the family can be together undisturbed and talk about our mother, remembering her long and colourful life.

Christof phones to ask me to put one red rose in her hand. He says it is very important, and so I go down to the chapel. No one is there. It is quiet, scented from the flowers, and filled with light and warmth. I put a rose in her hand. She lies in smiling peace, elegant, golden and still very close to her body, only distilled as far as the width and breadth and height of the chapel.

Supper is a party. All the cousins, the parents, but not
the babies! What a blessing baby-phones can be. And
what a blessing Rob is such a handyman. He found a phone
that transmits perfectly for up to a mile. So the babies
can sleep in their cots contentedly, and we can be with
them, down the few hundred yards, in a second should
they need us. We laugh and remember other family dos, in
which Mother presided as matriarch of the clan.

26 May

We have all slept well. We feel subdued, but happy.
Everyone goes to the service, I stay home and cook a
massive Sunday lunch because, after all, it is now my
house and I am the hostess. I feel Mother's presence,
approving of my generosity. It's strange not to be
listening out for her call, not needing to give her a
drink, fetch her knitting, lift her stool. Whilst
things simmer, I go out and start planting the flowers I
bought into the garden. The smell of wet earth and the
sound of the birds are like food to my soul. I imagine I
am tending a much richer garden, and that comforts me.

We are a family of singers. Mother had chosen the
songs she wanted for her funeral, so I organize a choir
practice to coincide with the last arrivals of sons and
cousins.

Agnes, Liz and I go to see Mother. We have suddenly
found some time-out from entertaining or organizing.
We want some time alone with her.

Her mouth has opened! She looks quite comical,
contrary to her usual dignity. Something must be done.
She would hate it if people saw her looking so silly. We
laugh a bit, trying to have practical ideas.

I go home and get from my crystal collection a small

clear plastic stand that jewellers use to prop up sliced agate. It is just the right height to push up her chin! We cover it with a pink rose and giggle irreverently. I have phoned the undertaker who comes later and fixes it properly. So instead of sitting quietly with her, as we had hoped, we are busy again, keeping things neat and tidy!

While we make tea for the next visitors, Liz puts the last of the plants into the garden and we walk round admiring our work. Mother will be happy to see that things look nice for all the people who have arranged to attend her funeral.

We spend the evening with the priest, telling him her life story, trying to pick out the moments that mattered most to her and to us. What a remarkable life she had, fearful, courageous, challenging, disciplined, hard and enlightening, inspiring and loving. So many, many people are who they are today because our mother gave to them a part of herself, without obligation and as a free gift of love.

27 May

Like all Mondays, this one starts with business. Rob goes for all the official papers and we book the crematorium. Mother wants her body to be burned up. (I will most certainly want to be buried!) We discuss each other's choices, giggling and having a lot of different ideas.

We start looking at photos, get lost in memories, interspersed with visitors who come to offer their condolences. The day is turning into a long party!

We try to sit with Mother in the chapel, bringing inner peace towards her soul, but not once can we be

Three sisters at the funeral. Left to right: Agnes, Liz and me

alone with her. Visitors flock in, apologize for
disturbing us, but they stay anyway, serious and
pious. I love to see how many people were touched by her
life. And we have been used to sharing her. All our
life, whenever we wanted to be just the family
together, someone would come, knock on the door and
want to see 'Barbara, just for a little moment'. Mother
would invite them in very warmly and give them her full
attention. We learned that a person in need should
never be turned away, so we do not mind these
interruptions. It is a fitting tribute to our mother's
life on earth.

The others have tea, and I go to a meeting to help
arrange a memorial evening. So many people have come
from all over the world that we want to give them a
chance to speak about our mother as they knew her, and
share what she meant to them. It exhausts me, I am not
fit to be efficient.

The last sons arrive, Marty (my youngest),
Matthew(Liz's second child) and David (Agnes's only
boy),and we start rehearsing the choir. It soars to the
skies. We feel her listening from above and beyond and
sing like larks.

We sing madrigals, and four-part songs by Arcadelt,
Schütz, Tallis. The harmonies ring out and across to
the other side, echoes of heavenly harmonies. It is
great fun and we laugh and dispute over
interpretation.

Finally everyone has gone to bed. Marty and I sit at
the kitchen table with a glass of wine and he tells me of
his journey over to Ireland.

Things were complicated so he left late. He drove
along a narrow road, and got stuck behind a lorry. A
motor cyclist overtook them, the lorry stopped. Marty
— impatient as always — got out to look, not able to
pass. In the road lay the cyclist. A car with an elderly
woman driver was also in the road, the motor bike in the
ditch. The lorry driver sat in shock. Marty sent the
woman to her house, from the driveway of which she had
emerged to knock down the cyclist. The lorry driver got
out, they rang the police and Marty did what he could to
help the cyclist — who died as the police arrived. The
man was only in his thirties.

Arriving late at the airport, Marty had missed his
flight. He had a first class ticket (the only one he
could get at such short notice) so could book onto the
next flight and then sleep in the business club lounge!
That expensive ticket had paid off and now it stood him
in good stead.

Marty sits opposite me, looking pale and shocked.
From one dying to another death, he says. But how

different is the dying of an old person from a young
one.

28 May

We wake early. Everyone appears dressed neatly, men in
suits. Marty wears a peculiar checked shirt and yellow
tie, quite unlike yesterday's sober clothes. I refrain
from commenting that his grey suit is the only
appropriate article he is currently wearing! He looks
tired so I hold my tongue. What would Mother have said?
He apologizes for his clothing, explaining that his more
sober outfit has blood on it from yesterday's accident.
We go to the chapel, which is already pretty full of
mourners gazing sternly into Mother's coffin. We go in
and smile, at her and at them. Some return the greeting,
others look slightly shocked at our evident joy.

We have had a superb run-through of music. Other
people than family have joined, young people who knew
our mother and loved her, old friends who arrived in
time to learn the songs. The music soared and I saw my
mother far away, huge and shining, up beyond the
ceiling of the music room, which had vanished into the
light of the other side. It is the music that has lifted
our souls.

Theo and Corneel take care of Helen Barbara. She,
being deaf, cannot join the singing, Theo won't sing,
and Corneel is on call for the babies who don't attend,
so they sit with her. Things just fall into place.
Elizabeth is the only child present. She stays in the
lobby with Tony. She sits on his arm looking serious,
pretty and behaving very well. The chapel is packed.
The priest's sermon is moving in the extreme, because
he has collected our stories, his memories and

Mother's history and made a biography of her true inner self. Her being shines through in every word, her courage, her striving, her commitment to serve humanity, her care of the disabled, her love of her husband, and her complete selflessness towards her children. We can see her as she truly was, a moral, kind, upright, courageous little woman, against whom the dark powers had small opportunity for damage.

Periodically, throughout the sermon, we hear the cheerful high tones of Elizabeth's voice, saying 'hiya!' She is flirting with the undertaker. His serious professional demeanour creases into a smile. The young and the old, new life on both sides of the river, converge in the chapel.

People file past the coffin to pay their last respects. Mother lies serene as the queen that she always was in later years. One of the crowd, an autistic girl, sheds noisy dramatic tears, behaving oh so appropriately, so taken by her own excellent performance that she goes to the back of the queue and files past again, hanky in hand, pressing it to her dry eyes with true artistry! We cannot help laughing, having to muffle it for fear of offending.

Throughout the singing, sermon and service, two large bumble-bees crawl round and round the coffin, threading their clumsy path between the masses of flowers. Their humming provides a low and natural bass for speech and music.

Outside the sun radiates light through the chapel windows onto the coffin. Then, as the short service ends, the clouds pile up, the light changes and it begins to pour with rain, thundering onto the copper roof over our heads.

The elements are here too. Nature spirits come to pay their respects with us! The members of the choir sing like angels, no false tones, faces serious. People leave, the family stay to close the coffin. We have asked Christof, the child she loved and cared for so many years ago, in another lifetime, to be the sixth bearer. We cannot help smiling as the six men juggle with differing heights, but finally she can be borne solemnly out of the chapel through the waiting crowd lining the path to the hearse, the women of the family following suitably slowly and solemnly.

I bear in my head and eyes the last sight of her, a golden little body, silver crowned, smiling in her Sunday dress, ready for her new life and entirely at peace with the world. I can hardly think what life will be like without her physical presence because I feel her so close to us, watching every move and setting her lips in approval or disapproval as the ceremony advances.

Two buses take us all to the crematorium. (She wouldn't have approved of this, maybe, but one must be practical and we need to keep the 30-strong choir together.) It feels like a Sunday school outing!

The staff at the crematorium come round afterwards. What, they ask, do you people believe in? We've never had such a joyful funeral before. The music was superb! One doesn't hear such singing often. I tell them we were always a singing family and that death is a crossing from one life to another. They smile a bit uneasily and go away.

People pass by to offer condolences, a never-ending stream. We three sisters stand and smile and smile and smile! So many wonderful people, all who loved our mother because she loved them. What a valedictory!

Now it's party time. Our neighbours have sent in food, and we gather in my mother's house (now mine) and eat, drink, and remember in merriment. Then some of us go to prepare the hall for her memorial evening. We bring all the flowers from the chapel and the hall is full, redolent with roses and lilies. The memorial evening is lovely. Streams of people reminisce about our mother, most telling of the wonderful way she supported them through times of trial. Each says she had been a mother to them. Just to create the balance, because such praise can be cloying, there were those who told of her strong temper, that she was a stickler for the details, everything had always to be done 'properly'.

Outstanding was the tribute from one of her grandsons, David, humorous and loving. He says his first memory of his grandmother was at the airport. While waiting for her he saw people pushing their luggage trolleys, but none was grandmother. But then a trolley emerged by itself. This One Was Grandmother! The littlest lady he had ever seen. One other tribute stays with me. The friend who arrived on Saturday (too late to see her after all) remembers her always as someone who, on parting, would look at you piercingly and say, Be well — a blessing given for the rest of one's life, to be well, do well and live well.

Now we have an Irish wake till the early hours, just the family. Baby-phones are so useful! We drink wine and laugh each other into sleep.

I am alone at last, outside on my bench, 2 o'clock in the morning, one last cigarette.

Mother stands in the garden, 50 years old, wearing

her grey dress, elegant, slim and smiling. She is in deep conversation with a being who towers over her, white light lapping lovingly around her, the wings of her angel a living caress, and she is answering with radiating white light. Clearly they are of one mind and one heart.

Later, in my bed, I wake out of sleep to the sound of her deathly groaning, but it is only a shadow image, still lingering in the bricks and mortar of the house. Her bright reality is moving onward into the light.

29–31 May

One by one, family and visitors depart. The phone ceases to ring incessantly. The silence is surging in, gradually filling the house with peace. The three sisters and two husbands are left to clear up. Only Jonathan, Liz's husband still in Australia, is missing. I am unspeakably tired. The euphoria is fading leaving exhaustion in its wake. The others, too, start to flag, but needs must, and there are some things still to be done. We go with Helen Barbara to collect Mother's ashes. She needs to see everything to understand it properly.

The supervisor at the crematorium wants to talk to us. He hands the plain wooden, unvarnished box of remains to Helen Barbara and says: We think of death as you do, as a joyful moment of release. But it is rare to meet others like us. We try to fill this place with light and warmth and flowers, but you have filled it also with music.

We are greatly touched by his gratitude. He says all the staff flocked to the door to listen to the singing and the service.

We eat a pub lunch and go to Mother's favourite country park for a walk. We are so tired we sit down in a row on a bench in the sun overlooking the lake and fall asleep!

The shimmering garden around us transforms into the other side. Mother is gone, the light is still surging happily, but there is no one to be seen. The dark shadow in the corner is a little darker and stronger, as though calling me, but I refuse to look. The river is dark, slow and silent. The path up the incline of the mountain is empty but for the distant indication of a person, though I cannot make out who it is. I feel enormously comforted. My mother has gone, into the light.

We shop for thank-you cards, make lists of those whom we need to contact, mull over the last few days and sleep in between.

We search for a suitable tree to put on her grave. We cannot decide what to choose. In the end, we take a cutting of root from the sandthorn tree outside the house. She wanted a tree that would feed the birds! It is a humble, wild and undemanding tree, not pretty but sturdy and reliable.

We realize that as I have inherited her house, Rob and I are now the family's physical centre. But I am the youngest and cannot take her place at all! Agnes is the real centre of our 'tribe' now. We laugh at such silly things, but the truth is we all love this spot on earth and I will try to be a good guardian of it. I am after all only here by default, so I will have to serve in my role very well.

We look at Mother's jewelry, share it out.

Erika comes to help sort out her private papers.

Mother left a letter requesting this. We eat supper together, a peaceful adult meal — no more babies and children and grandchildren except Elizabeth, who comes every day to see me. Now I truly feel a grandmother, since my mother is gone.

Tony digs the grave-hole for the little box. The weather is mild, the air is still and a kind of silence, an inner tranquility, hangs over the chapel garden.

Later, we buy some azaleas. They remind me of the branches someone (we never found out who) put in Mother's room when she came home from hospital. I feel strangely comforted as I dig them into the garden beside the sandthorn tree under Mother's window. Death is part of nature's cycle, and planting is part of making this a reality.

1 June

The memorial service is wonderful. Not many people come, but all those who attend were dear to Mother, and she dear to them. There is hardly any music. A peaceful inwardness pervades the chapel.

Helen Barbara has carried the urn from the house with reverence and love, like a mother holding a baby. Now she takes it out to the hole in the wet ground and we stand in a wide circle ready for the burial. As she kneels to place the box, there is a rush of wings overhead.

Look! Look at the geese! We look up. Over the circle of mourners wings a perfect formation of wild geese, one single goose up ahead as leader, leaving one leg of the V shorter. Honking deliciously and raucously, they swoop over our heads and shoot off, flying from west to east in an arrow of purpose.

With them we send an upsurge of joy, everyone laughing and smiling in farewell. Be well! We hear her call from the other side.

Part Three

THE GOLD

After my mother died, the way to the other side seemed to be wide open. I went to and fro frequently, sometimes unexpectedly, but often deliberately. For some time after she had crossed, I saw the garden, empty of people, the light gently billowing and moving, and in the forefront a high stone arch. It stood freely, without supports, made of building stones as one sees over the doorways of old Celtic churches, the cut and angle of the stones that form the arch being their only support. It was quite solid and strong and through the arch I saw the light, brighter and more concentrated. It was entirely clear to me that she had passed through this very archway with her own angel. Was this why she said before the end: 'The door is open'? However, I saw no door, only the arch. It made me smile to see it standing all alone without the usual attendant building. The position of this gateway was precisely where the bunker had been at the death of those whom the suicide bomber hit.

I began to think about how being close to someone who is dying can be very different for different people. It occurred to me, rather obviously, that I was privileged to be travelling with my mother on her journey into life. Here on earth, for almost 90 years, she had led her destiny in a most remarkable way. Usually, we are led by our destiny, but my mother took her fate and shook it into obedience to her spirit-filled will.

My Mother's Life Story

Barbara, as we knew her to be called, had not always been so named. She was born into a Jewish Hasid family in Poland who fled to Vienna to escape the pogroms at the beginning of the twentieth century. She was quite different from the rest of her family, being blond and blue eyed and not looking Jewish at all. A photograph of her with her family at the age of three shows a serious, pretty child, a ribbon in her straight hair revealing a broad, high forehead and a determined mouth, held firmly closed. Her expression is one that says: 'Do we have to sit here much longer? If so, I will be patient for as long as it takes!' This little girl was called Sali, or Surali, in the Yiddish that her family and relatives used, though she herself never spoke anything but good high German with a slight Austrian lilt, much to her family's amazement. Already as a small child, she was an individual.

Her mother was rather unpractical, and her father devoted his time to his religious worship, rather than earning their bread and butter. Sali tried to create a clean and tidy home, always longing for beauty. When she was still very young, she fell on the cobbles of the streets in which they played so enthusiastically, and hurt her knee. It did not heal and caused her terrible pain. Eventually they diagnosed TB in the joint and she had to wear a caliper to keep her knee rested. Her sisters took her out and about with them as usual, in an old pram, but the laughing child who loved to run and skip and jump was now an invalid. Nights and days were filled with pain, and sleep became a far distant luxury. Sometimes the piano music of the cinema above which they lodged drove her mad. At other times, her father's incessant prayer-chanting was her torture. She cried out to him one afternoon: 'Father, please stop praying!' He ignored her and went on chanting. She was consumed by enormous anger and despair. How could the God of her father want him to disturb a child in pain? She experienced her first rejection of Judaism aged nine, wondering if there could be a God somewhere whose mission taught love.

Because of her illness, she could not go to school. Her sisters brought her books and she devoured them, learning from the great masters such as Goethe and Schiller. The ancient masters of fairy-tales also accompanied her studies. She read her sisters' maths, physics, chemistry, geography and history books and so could leave school years later complete in her education.

She was sent on cures to the Adriatic by the social workers of her day because she came from an underprivileged family. These places were run by Catholic nuns. Now she found a religion of light and music, of colour and vision. She attended mass every day, knowing even at the age of nine that this would not be sanctioned by her father's sombre faith. She understood not a word — the services were held in Latin — but the imagery stayed with her, even after her parents took her away. She felt she had found a well of light and joy.

In her teens, she decided she wanted to be a kindergarten teacher, perhaps because her own childhood had been so decisively cut short, but it was necessary for any would-be teacher to obtain a good pass in physical education. So she went to the Minister for Education in Vienna, sat in his waiting-room, and demanded an interview. He granted her special dispensation from the examination and she went on to follow her calling.

Furthermore, she had discovered a surgeon who could do something about her diseased knee. Following her usual pattern, she sat day after day in his waiting-room until he agreed to see her. He assured her he could operate, but this would mean stiffening the knee permanently and shortening her leg. She agreed to this, but informed him that she had no money at present to pay for the surgery required. However, she would sign an IOU and repay him by instalments. The doctor did the operation and refused to charge her. Now she could walk again without pain but her knee was straightened so she could no longer kneel. With head held high, she resolved to find humility in another way.

Sali had a brother who suffered from epilepsy as well as learning difficulties. He was, as she phrased it, 'a charming, impossible child'. They did not understand his needs. Sali took him on, though she too felt utterly ill-equipped for the job. And so finally, unable to carry on with him, he was put into a large mental hospital, where he died of pneumonia just before Hitler annexed Austria. Sali mourned him greatly, feeling she had failed his evident need.

She had in the meantime become acquainted with the work of Rudolf Steiner. She found his teaching exciting and challenging, feeling something in her ideals coming alive. She had also come to know a doctor, the man who helped her with her epileptic brother. He too was a follower of Rudolf Steiner. She brought her friends to meet this clever, inspiring doctor, and study groups arose in which she said she felt like the only practical person in the room, the rest being philosophers, doctors, lawyers and other learned people. She became the nanny for the doctor's children, one of whom was Christof. The doctor wanted to found a community focused on the needs and education of handicapped children. When her brother died, they were in the middle of a social exercise aimed at learning to work together. As a balance to their studies, the doctor had decided to rehearse and perform a Christmas play with them all.

Sali had embraced the Christian faith, as had most of the members of their study group. Her parents were horrified, declaring her to be beyond their understanding and also a traitor. Visits home were painful. They judged her cruelly, but her youngest brother, who was studying to become a rabbi, often talked to her, telling her that the Jewish faith too knew of other spiritual beings and another life than this one on earth. Why did she need to look to Christianity for a spiritual path? At the end of her life, she remembered these conversations with love and longing, because her beloved brother died in the Holocaust that Hitler wrought and could not bring to full fruition his religious knowledge and feelings. She wondered what he would have become, he who found reincarnation within the Jewish faith, the world of angels and archangels, and the transformation of the material into spiritual substance.

But, she added, that way was not for her. She found her path through following the teaching of Christ and by the work of Rudolf Steiner. One must be true to one's conscience, was commonly on her lips when confronted with decisions.

And so, when her handicapped brother died, Sali was learning the part of Mary, the mother of the Jesus child in the Christmas play. She wanted to go to her family to mourn his death. The good doctor forbade her to go, saying that if she did so she would interrupt the holy task she had taken of playing Mary. He would not allow her to undertake the role if she disobeyed him. Sali was astounded, and then angry. Quietly, she packed a weekend bag and went to her family to mourn her brother. She would follow her conscience always, not loudly and with pomp and circumstance, but quietly and with dedication.

She escaped the concentration camps by fleeing to England. The others in the circle around the doctor also came to Britain. They began to establish a base in order to develop their dedication to the handicapped as a means of expressing their commitment to life, whilst the rest of the world went to war against the power of darkness that arose through Hitler's dominion. But Sali had other commitments to fulfil before she could join her friends who were already setting up a home for children in need of special care in Scotland. No doubt she could have made excuses to the family whose children she had agreed to care for. But this was not her way. She had taken on a task and would follow her heart only when the task was completed.

When she was finally free to join her friends, a community was slowly brought into being, led strongly by the doctor and his wife. Its central aim was to work through curative education as taught by Rudolf Steiner, and to match this outer work with inner spiritual development. In the midst of such a novel endeavour Sali felt that she needed a new name. She took the name of Barbara, which means 'the stranger'.

She met and married a man whose character was as outgoing as hers was inward. He was remarkably clever and challenging, but before long he suffered a head injury which left him disabled in many ways. Barbara, carrying their first child, had made a commitment to him in marriage and saw no reason to relinquish it. She helped him to learn as much as he could to return as closely as possible to normality. Her love and respect for this damaged man shone through to us as children. We always knew our father needed a particular approach, but we never once saw him as handicapped. We respected and loved him through the eyes and heart of our mother.

My Mother's Inner Life

Barbara, outwardly a small woman, with a stiffened knee and shortened leg, set out to meet her life's work. She used to say all too often: 'I am not clever, like all the others. I am just a simple woman and not good at learning.' She confused 'intellect' with 'intelligence'. She was highly intelligent in the ways of the heart. Her powers of accurate observation were always led by her feeling, softening the intellect into real understanding for human nature. She chose as her contribution to the growing community, now springing up all over the world, to devote herself to the small things in life.

She loved everything: cooking, cleaning, washing, nursing, caring and protecting. Whatever she handled she touched with love. Her hands were always gentle, worn and sometimes the skin was raw from hard work. She could make beautiful flower bunches, bake wonderful cakes and bread. She darned clothes and her ironing was immaculate. Watching her dealing with the stuff of ordinary life was like watching someone perform a holy deed. She made her work into her prayer.

Her relations to her fellow community members were as courageous as her deeds were modest. If something needed to be said, she would say it — fearlessly following her conscience. And so she grew to be a tower of strength for many, many people, because she became truly wise. She would listen to a problem, her eyes fixed on the face of the speaker, and then proffer something simple in response, something that the hearer could take away and actually apply. Her wisdom came from daily life.

Barbara had her little sins, however. She was immensely vain, her vanity expressing itself in the clothes she wore. They had to be hand-made and must be neat and tidy. At table, the décor must be beautiful and precise. She hated carelessness and mess. She wore beautiful jewelry, simple in form, but always of real gemstones and gold or silver. She despised costume jewellery and anything artificial. She transformed her vanity into creating beauty over all things. When one visited her, her room was always neat, everything placed just so that its inner value and outer beauty were at their best. One felt at home in her presence because one felt 'seen' as an outer as well as an inner person. But woe betide anyone if they were dressed carelessly or spoke carelessly of things or people. She would tighten her mouth and straighten her back, often in very subtle movements, and one would feel reproved, an unworthy specimen of human endeavour. As a younger person, her disapproval would be quite directly and verbally expressed!

The one thing that made her truly angry was a lie. However horrible the truth might be it was always better than a lie. Her search for, and honour of, the truth led her to be truthful in herself. When she knew she was dying and no one would say it out loud, her depression overcame her like a cloud. As soon as she was clear about her illness, she became filled with light. The little daily demons still plagued her during her illness but she fought them off bravely, with patience and humour. Throughout her life, she was often ruthless, with herself and with others, if any slothfulness appeared in one's striving for self-development. To shirk one's immediate responsibilities was a cardinal sin in her eyes. And if someone were to complain about how hard their life was, she would say gently: 'We all get what we deserve. We never get more than we can bear.'

She believed that modesty was the greatest virtue. She, who could never kneel physically, knelt daily inwardly in disciplined attempts to meditate. She said, towards the end of her life, that she had never learned really to meditate. But she had learned to pray. And as her hearing and then her sight failed her, she took to praying for the world as her inner task, her small commitment to lighting up the world.

Her leader and guide was the Archangel Michael. Though she was never called upon to fight outer dragons, she fought the small, seemingly insignificant ones of dirt and carelessness and daily little lies. When she struggled to leave her body at the end, all her fusses and complaints were endearing. Inwardly she held fast to the truth, that she was moving from this material world to the world of light and life. She was grateful for every little thing done for her. She was a good companion till the last.

She used to say to me, when I got impatient with life's little irritations: 'You must accept! Only by accepting your destiny will you be able to lead it on. Resentment is the worst sin. Search for the truth within your life, within whatever comes towards you, and this will give you strength for living.'

By her commitment to accept her destiny, she transformed her vices into virtues. Not that she was at any time a holier-than-thou person. She rolled her sins through the mill-wheel of daily life, and ground them into fine flour to be baked into the bread of life. Though she struggled to understand what meditating really was, and said she couldn't really do anything with it, she never gave up. She worked hard to be able to see beyond this material world, accepting that a spiritual world existed, without being able to prove it. Her faith became eternal and very humble.

She once confided to me that as a child and young woman she had often been very afraid. She was afraid of the dark, of strangers abducting her, because in the neighbourhood where she grew up this happened almost nightly to young girls. Lying dying in her itching body, she fought that fear, struggling bravely to reach for the light.

Barbara's conscience was her guide and master. She listened to its voice and followed it wherever it might lead her. She had, when her conscience dictated, a lion's courage. One could not lie to her, because her inner voice found the deception instantly. In her old age, she learned to listen to her heart and soften the strident commands of her conscience into love for human frailties.

The Loneliness of Dying

I got to know my mother so much better by being part of her dying. The companionship became so precious. While she was in hospital, she withdrew from me, going into a world of her own in order, I thought, to blot out the misery within its walls. It was indeed a miserable place, not for lack of good will, because the nurses and doctors did their very best, but for lack of under-standing of life beyond life. A hospital's function is to save physical life. When that proves to be impossible, its function ceases to be fruitful. There is no further use for it, so one just waits for the end to come, seeing to it that the body doesn't suffer too much. Hospitals were not created to nurse the soul and spirit into another life!

Opposite my mother's bed lay an old lady who was clearly demented. She continuously called the nurse to take her to the toilet, groaning and cursing. If they did not come when she called, she rolled out of bed onto the floor, hurting herself. So they put up sides to her bed. Then she struggled to her knees and called them, cursing, all day long. At night, they gave her sleeping pills to silence her cries. No one visited her, no one sat with her, she just called and cried. When I went to talk to her, she slapped me. Eventually, some social workers came to take her to a nursing home, as her illness could not be cured. I hoped she would be befriended there, until her crossing time.

Next to her lay another woman, in a coma. She did not eat or drink, except when her son visited. He was large and balding, and rather lacking in personal hygiene. He sat beside her, held her hand and talked to her, about what a good mother she had been, how he loved her, how he would miss her, how life would be terrible without her to keep peace between him and his brother, how his brother hurt him when he was a child. I could not help overhearing because he spoke very loudly. When he sat by her, she stirred, swallowed some lurid orange drink, and seemed happier. When he left her, she withdrew again.

Her other son also came to visit. He wore a suit and seemed more prosperous than his brother. He sat by her side, not speaking, got up restlessly to walk about the day room, and cornered the busy nurses, demanding to know what was wrong with his mother and what they were doing about it. He never stayed very long. One day, both brothers were there together. A great row erupted, they shouted at each other, and the nurses came and took them away. The old woman lay unconscious, silent, in a foetal position, after they had gone. The next day her bed was empty, made up neatly for a new occupant. I asked where she had gone. The lady beside my mother said that they had moved her to a side ward. I asked the nurses the next day how she was, and they said, with embarrassed faces, that she had passed away. They also asked me not to speak so loudly about her death as this would upset the other patients.

One afternoon, a wheelchair stood in the day room in front of the TV. The programme running on it was some sort of chat-show. In the chair lay the crumpled form of an old woman. Her white hair was uncombed and she was wearing a washed-out nightdress. She lay calling softly and helplessly: 'Help me. Help me.' She kept on saying this, and when I asked her what she wanted she just said: 'Help me.'

I called the nurse and she said cheerfully: 'Oh, she always says that. It doesn't mean anything.'

The next day, the woman wasn't there, but I heard one of the nurses saying: 'Thank God she's gone.'

The loneliness of some crossings must be very hard. No wonder some people are so distressed when they wake up on the other side! But it made me very, very happy to have the knowledge and the opportunity to do things perhaps a little more humanly for my mother. There is no doubt in my mind that my mother's attitude towards life here on this side opened the way for me to accompany her, at least in part, with clear eyes and ears. Her last words, 'The door is open', were spoken clearly and softly, as though she was so glad to be allowed to walk through. The arch that I now saw must have surrounded that door, invisible because she had gone through at last.

Gates of Birth and Death

Eventually the arch faded away and the garden returned to its state of living beauty. My visits became less frequent. I wondered about that, and I wondered again why I was able to cross over so easily during my mother's dying and why it was becoming gradually less frequent and more difficult. Then I noticed that in my immediate vicinity we had had a year of births and deaths. Nine babies were born in the 18 months surrounding my mother, and my mother-in-law's death. And 26 people to whom I was connected had died. Not all of them had I seen, but clearly the path to the other side and the gate of birth and death were very wide open. I wondered if this was the reason for the gift of seeing so clearly?

When my father died, years earlier, I did not have any access to the event. He had been a gardener for most of his life, and was a wonderful story-teller. He died suddenly, of a heart attack, and he crossed over laughing gloriously at a joke he had just made. To me, he was gone, and I cried bitterly at his funeral. I felt that having escaped the concentration camp ovens, his body was now being cremated after all. I could not stay in the room, and rushed out of the nearest door, finding myself in the garden of the crematorium. It was January, and very cold, the sky grey with heavy rain clouds. At that moment of deepest distress, the clouds opened and a bright dazzling beam of sunlight travelled to the earth and in that beam, a lark soared up, singing its heart out to the invisible sun. I was stunned to silence, my tears dried up, and I felt immensely comforted by this strange natural display.

For three years, I was cut off from my father, but the memory of the sunbeam and the lark-song kept me going. Then one day, as I sat in my living room, I felt his hand take hold of mine. I had not been thinking about him at all, but nevertheless, there was his large warm hand, skin callused and cracked from gardening, the roughness and warmth embracing my fingers and palm. I was quite content after that, and have known him to be a part of my life ever since.

How different was my mother's passing, and how different was my involvement! Only gradually I grew to realize what had been happening. I was accompanying my mother through her soul and spirit experiences as her body was loosening its hold upon her. And I could see clearly what she could not recognize or put into words. Because my mother had devoted her life to lifting up the ordinary daily life experiences through the exercising of her conscience, she had not been able herself always to see what her spirit underwent. It is often hard to recognize one's own wisdom. And because she knew she was vain, she always modestly pushed any other-world experience into the ranks of imagination rather than seeing them as the forming of images of the spiritual world.

On the other hand, she was devoted to nature spirits, willing to call on them. She was strongly connected to angels, willing to work with them. She was deeply drawn to human endeavour, willing to encourage it. But towards herself she humbly ignored any steps she herself took, leaving that up to the spiritual world to acknowledge. In this way, what she saw as her greatest weakness she turned into her greatest strength.

Because I loved her, I was obliged throughout the weeks of her dying to devote myself to her as she had so often devoted herself to me. So we were bound together on the journey to the other side. Why did I never tell her what I saw? With hindsight, I think she would not have wanted to be told. She needed to do things in her own way, and I in mine.

I have only seen my mother once since she died. I was walking to a meeting, one that I knew would be decisive for our community and its future development, and I was worried about how things would work out. I saw her, huge above the clouds, wings outspread and moving with the sighing wind, her hair fine as always and smoothed back to lie against the shape of her skull. Her eyes were gazing far into the distance, and her form dissolved into the cloud formation, like sinking into a still lake. She had apparently no legs, and could fly high over the land. I felt such a wave of blessing raining down onto us all.

The Impact of Group Deaths

One evening, in the summer of the year in which she died, I found myself thrown into the garden on the other side. I felt quite winded, having been so suddenly taken over the river. I saw a pilot in uniform, hat at an angle, gazing up and around in perplexity, a little flustered. All around I heard children's voices, laughing delightedly, and behind that delicious joy, the sound of the wind blowing like rushing water. The light surged and moved, dancing with the children's voices, and the man stood puzzled and confused.

The joy uplifted me, and when I went inside to wash the supper dishes, the phone rang. A friend from Germany called to tell me she had seen a plane crash overhead. She was still in shock, stammering and distressed. A Russian charter plane exploded as it hit a freight plane, which also disintegrated in a burst of flames. The debris had fallen all around her house, and the police were sealing off the area to look for children's bodies. They had been going to Spain as a reward for excellent school results.

I watched the news on the television, stunned by the tragedy that to my experience was such a happy event. The voices of the children still rang in my ears, now parallel with the distress of their families that were shown on the television. Why had I been witness to their crossing? Was it because the pilot was so shocked and confused at the suddenness of his death?

I went over again, to see whether I could help him, but he was gone, only a kind of shadow of his presence still filling the place where he had stood on the living green grass. But I prayed for him, hoping this would be of help. And the dark area in the distance was darker than before, the pull to go and investigate very much stronger. However, I really did not want to know what it was and resisted the call. After this event, I saw no one on my visits, which happened daily, usually after breakfast. I knew there were people in the garden because the light kept changing formation, but I saw no one specifically.

Again, a few weeks later, as I stood in the garden on the other side, I heard children's joyful laughter, and this time I saw bodies lying indented into the green of the garden. I thought: 'Has there been another air disaster, or is this a repeat of the Russian plane that crashed?' So I turned on the news and heard of the Ukrainian air show, and saw the pictures of the aircraft hurtling to the ground, bits of metal flying around, and the people running screaming from the scene. The two worlds united, what I saw on the television and the sounds of laughter and chatter that filled my inner ear. The light beings were bending solicitously over indentations in the grass of the garden, but I could not make out particulars. I was filled with the warmth and joy of the other side and the distress here on this side.

For the next few days I pondered on the discrepancy between what we know here in life and what we block from our waking consciousness. Can we know of continued life after crossing the river? Can it only be known by a few lucky people? How does one come to be one of those fortunate few? And then I realized something else.

The Death of Children and That of Adults

Those who have become adults on this side before crossing can be seen on the other side. They are so much more physical, have entered their material bodies so much more deeply. Children, however, are still filled with the light of their spirits and so they fly across into death with ease, and also with joy, straight into the embrace of the the their bright angels. I realized that apart from the little girl in Cambodia, I had always *heard* children, never seen them as I saw adults. And even the little girl announced herself first through my hearing, only later through my vision.

Is it because we enter so deeply into our bodies that we are prevented from knowing the reality of the other side? Our bodies are too dense, they need so much light to get up and walk about, to open the senses, to be alive, that the light is dimmed, used up purely for survival. But little children, and babies, are so delicate that the light can still illuminate the world of the spirit and so children can cross so much more easily than adults. We grieve more when a child dies, knowing they have not yet really lived, and rejoice more easily when an old person crosses over. But the reality from the other side is quite the opposite! Children can be received without a transition period of adjustment to their new existence, hence the sounds of laughter and feelings of joy. Whereas adults, especially young adults, who love life here in their bodies, need to be helped to make the change and this is harder work for the beings of light who wait for us in the garden. Old people who have transformed their material existence by striving to overcome their small sins reach the light in recognition, though they have to struggle a little to leave their clinging bodies.

Though this was some sort of answer to my question, I still felt I needed more understanding as to 'why me?' But in the meantime, I accepted my visits, was glad of their renewing power, and waited for perhaps a clearer answer to come. I had not yet tried to force any issue with the other side, because that never brought any success. I had learned that wanting achieved only blankness.

I would have to simply be open, to wait for whatever would come next.

Friends Who Meet Us on the Other Side

The summer passed and autumn approached. The leaves were turning half-heartedly because of a surprisingly warm sun, but the evenings were drawing in and the rooks came home. The rooks always come back from down the lough around September, wheeling and dipping at sunset, to roost in the trees that border our estate. Now they flocked, shrieking their raucous cry, black against the skyline. It was time for lighting fires and putting on a coat to sit on my bench outside my mother's now empty bedroom window.

I watched the rooks and saw the path winding up the steep hill to the river at the top. I could not see the river, though I knew it was there, but I walked along the path and saw the vegetation dying out towards the summit. Rocks appeared, dry, dusty and old. Up ahead of me, at the top I saw the tiny figure of a young woman, waiting. She was facing me, looking down the mountainside, waiting patiently for someone. I recognized her by her black fringed hair, Japanese style, and her make-up, very strong round the eyes. She is a friend who died many years ago, perhaps by her own hand.

Then I was on the other side, looking out over the river, now broad and slow moving, black and deep, and as I gazed down the mountain path, which wound steeply up towards the river, I saw, in the distance a black figure. I could make out no features and could only see the person doing a peculiar kind of jiggling dance reminiscent of tribal rites, hands up in the air and waving in rhythm to an inaudible tortured musical beat. It was so bizarre that I laughed. The prancing figure continued to gyrate madly, as though compelled, and I saw that the feet were in very high-heeled, tight, black and shiny patent-leather shoes. Then I recognized her. She was another friend, elderly, and the mother of the petite girl I had seen as I looked up to the river at the top of the mountain.

The rooks cawed again and I was once more on my bench, contemplating this weird scene. Why the agonizingly awkward dance? That she was approaching the river was not surprising, and that her daughter was waiting for her was also not surprising. This old lady would need someone she knew to welcome her, because she was convinced that death was the end of life, and would be completely surprised by her new life to come. Only a close companion that she could recognize would be able to help her to see clearly. But the dance was something new to me, as well as the appearance of the old lady already in a black silhouette before she had reached the further shore. Usually those I saw approaching the river were in dark clothing, but not that distinctive black opaqueness that I saw illuminated by the light once they had crossed. These were very new pictures.

I told my sister about all this, that the old lady was close to the river. She was not surprised, saying that from all outward signs this would be true. Could I, she asked, predict when she would cross? I had to admit that I could not. No one seems to take the same time as any other. Each sighting has, to date, been quite individual. I am not able to see the future, only the present. I am relieved at this, because that would be a great burden to carry, and already I am not sure why I see these things at all. I do not want to become a fortune-teller! However, we agreed to think of the old woman to give her strength for her journey to the river-crossing whenever the time will come.

Since then I have seen her often, moving slowly up the path, and usually I am walking with her, as she toils slowly in her impossible shoes, which as a young woman she loved to wear. Sometimes I see her from the other side, and lately she has stopped dancing madly and is walking more steadily. She is visibly in colour now, wearing a tight skirt and fashion blouse, beige and tan, and her shoes are soft flat, light brown suede with shining patent leather toe-caps, very chique. She is wearing red lipstick, which she always did when younger, liking to accentuate her figure and her mouth. Her hair is cut short, boyish and black, and she is looking very serious indeed, but not anxious any more. The daughter has gone, at least from my vision, but I feel her presence each time I see the old lady. She is still waiting for her.

Calling on Those Who Have Died Long Ago

I saw a touching confirmation of the reality that someone awaits us on the other side, if one's understanding of continued life is tentative and unsure. I woke up in the middle of the night and saw, sitting in a chair at the river bank, an old lady. She seemed to be asleep, her head resting on the chair back, her right arm dangling down over the armrest and almost touching the ground. I recognized her immediately, a woman whose disposition was soured by disappointment in life, a failed relationship and inability to raise her child lovingly. I saw that on the other side a man waited for her. He was her lover, the man she had wanted to marry but who had not after all matched her desire. He had died many years before her.

To say that I saw him is not quite accurate. I did not see him as I usually did, in form and focus. I saw him with an inner eye. He was huge, his boundary of being almost as vast as that of the light beings, and I knew he was struggling to shrink his beingness into a form that the woman, asleep on the other bank, would be able to recognize. He did this out of love, a love far different from what the woman understood love to be. His love embraced and healed, sending solace to all pain, need and grief.

Her love seemed tiny, a little spark of hope in the darkness. But that tiny spark had enough power to call him back from a place far away beyond the garden and the light that is our first consciousness when we cross over.

He was there, waiting for her to wake up. I saw them again, a few days later, she bewildered but happy, her hand touching his arm, her eyes glancing joyously at his beloved face. In life on earth, she judged he had failed her, but now she knew that his love went beyond what she could greedily grab for herself. He seemed to be telling her what she should look for now, and she listened, charmingly attentive. The light beings surged and moved, their brightness dazzling my vision, so much so that I saw no more, and was back here again. I was as happy as she was, to know that their painfully damaged earthly connection would find healing in the truth of their joint karma.

Healing After Death

Soon after this visit, we went on holiday to the sun, a winter infusion of warmth and light. I sat on the terrace, relaxed and warm, dozing. Then I stood by the river-bank, gazing across to the spot where the young man who died by drowning had crouched. I knew that spot, and could identify it in the same way as one recognizes a familiar landmark. The light was incredibly bright, moving in the most powerful of waves towards a black figure that danced the same strange dance as the old lady. I gradually made out that it was a Japanese man. I *knew* he was Japanese, but what gave me this information I cannot say. He jiggled in his black suit, his hair cut badly in a short-back-and-sides, the cap flattened off, so that the remaining tufts stood right up like a brush. His eyes were wide and startled and I could now see that this jiggling was brought on by agonizing pain of some sort. The feet danced and hopped and the arms waved in tortured movements.

Now I was in my usual place on the other side and could see the river, narrow, and slowly widening as the Japanese man danced out his pain. From within the surging light beings, a white light detached itself, revealing itself as a being of great beauty and harmony, graciously dimensioned, who approached the gyrating man from behind with warmth and love. The man danced on, heedless of the light and facing the broadening river, highly distressed.

From the dark shadow that I so dreaded to explore, there flowed towards us a blue flame. It moved serenely across the greenness of the garden as though floating. It grew taller and taller as it approached the man, shining with the blue glancing light that lies at the centre of a candle flame. It flickered and swirled and bent over the man, and he stood still. He appeared to have lost all movement and merely drooped by the river, whilst the white brightness and the blue flame conferred with one another, immensely loving and implacable too. The white light moved back towards the ocean of light and the blue flame 'shepherded' the Japanese man towards the darkness in the distance. I did not want to follow but was 'compelled' to do so.

To describe this compulsion is very difficult. It was not a force that moved me against my will. It was rather like the firm and loving hand of one's mother that guides one, willy-nilly, up the stairs to bed when one is a tired little child who wants to sleep but also wants to play a little longer. One can lean back on that gentle hand and make a bit of a token fuss, but actually one is grateful to go to bed. In this way, I too was 'shepherded' behind the Japanese man, towards the dark shadow, which I now saw was a 'building'.

Like a cave, yet fashioned out of living darkness, it opened up into a vast hollow, stretching back to its interior, indefinitely. I knew that it was real, a real cave for shelter, but that it was not hollowed out of a mountain but out of the substance – the very same substance that fashioned the garden. It shimmered and moved infinitely slowly, dark and solid, as the garden greenness was alive and gleaming.

I stood at the entrance and saw how the blue flame shepherded the man, with gentle gestures, to what appeared to be an open catafalque, oblong and empty, into which he climbed and lay down, instantly asleep. He had, in fact, fallen into this sleep as soon as the blue flame reached him, already in the garden. I knew this because the blue flame told me, as it explained to me all the rest of what followed. There were, of course, no words, but subtle and clear meaning flowed into me throughout this visit. The blue flame settled down at the head of the stone casket, as though on watch, with a gesture of its form that told of caring, loving nursing. I saw how the cave was filled with rows of these caskets, one beside the other, with a passage down the middle dividing them. The rows on either side stretched on and on. I could not see the end. Each casket on the left of the cave had its occupant and its own blue flame as nurse. Inside the caskets slept people, and I saw that there were no children there. Most were people in their middle years, some were elderly, and they were of neither sex, just people. They looked peaceful and inert.

To the right, the caskets were at a slightly lower level and the people who slept in them were less clearly visible to my eyes. There were no blue flames. Instead, the whole area glowed as if in embers of firelight. The warmth pulsated, filling the space with healing, glowing, gentle red light. The silence was extraordinary, resonating with the humming sound that only the movement of living light can make. I was told that here people lie who are in particular need of healing before they can see their angel lights.

I saw down the rows how the darkness of the cave began to grow lighter around a certain casket, that the roof grew thinner, and that the person lying asleep began to move softly. The blue flame at his head grew bigger and brighter, moving and bending almost in excitement. The person sat up, helped by the blue flame and looked up to the brightening, thinning roof. This opened, and in streamed a glowing angel welcoming the person, who raised his arms, as a child does to his mother, and got up to leave the cave with his angel. He went out at the end of the cave, where I knew it entered into eternity. I stood at the other end, at the mouth of the darkness of the cave, where the light of the garden could barely penetrate.

The darkness in the cave returned once the angel had left with his willing charge. The casket was empty only for a moment. Then I saw a new figure in black enter the cave, shepherded in by his blue flame, to lie down and sleep in the casket just vacated.

The mood in this vast cavern was like a hospital ward, or a sleeping nursery of children, row upon row, in peace. Though the love from the blue flames was all pervading, so was a sense of active waiting. The flames rose and fell in intensity of light, moving softly around the sleeping bodies. They seemed to be meditating their patients into health. And health was the waking to the light, to their own angel light.

I remembered the little Jewish man and the elderly friend of my mother's who met him, and how their lights were different colours, hers a brightness to gold, and his a brightness to silver. I saw that the Japanese man's light had also been silver in colour. Did these angelic colours have some meaning too?

As I thought this, I was again on the terrace in the sun, tired, and rejuvenated too. Now I understood the shadow in the distance that I had so strongly resisted. It is a hospital for those who cannot recognize that they have crossed into another life. Those who suffer ignorance of continuous life are considered ill on the other side, in need of special care, until they have woken to their new existence. The blue flames are the nurses, who administer their loving light as healing. No wonder there are no children!

Bathing in the River

For some time, I could no longer cross after visiting the hospital. The door was firmly shut, and whenever I tried to make the journey the same compelling sensation came to me as it had when I was propelled to the cave. Clearly something was wanted of me. I was not shown the dark shelter for nothing. I had not wanted to be shown, but I could not resist the force that took me there. Now something was being asked of me, but I did not know what it was. So once again, I waited, open to what might come. But crossing over now seemed to be banned.

And then the way opened again. I was told of the dying of a great friend, a doctor who had cared for me as a child, and for my own three children. She was no longer conscious of this world. She lay in her bed, not eating or drinking, and so we thought she would die very soon. For her I could visit again! But when I was there, on the other side, I could not see her at all, only the elderly lady in her beige outfit, who was wandering along the river bank, a small smile on her red lips, as though looking for a good place to cross.

The week went by, the doctor was still here. I sat outside and saw the river again, broad and deep and I saw the doctor, about 25 years old, wearing a 1920s swim suit with arms and legs of black knitted cloth. Slim and beautiful, she dived into the river. And she swam there! Quite happily, under water, bathing in the depths of the living moving waters, between the two worlds.

Here on this side she was unconscious in her bed, neither alive nor dead for nearly three weeks. I knew she had finally made it because on the day she died, several hours before I was informed of her death, I saw the light give a great shouting upsurge of fire. I did not see the doctor herself, however, as she must have risen from the river's waters into the waiting angelic world. But they were more than glad to receive her.

The Meaning of Grief

Since that time, I have rarely been able to return in the same way. I feel the nearness of the other side as a constant living companion, and part of me longs to go there again. When I wake to the day's sunlight, I see the natural world with a greater brilliance, penetrated by light that lives within the sunlight but is not material light. Nature has a sheen that it did not have before. Colours are brighter, more alive, and the shape and texture of things in nature are more vivid to the touch. There is sustenance and peace and joy over there, which penetrates and weaves in nature over here. And thus I have come to understand what is wanted from me through having been allowed to cross over so freely.

The blue flames, which heal those who cross in ignorance of the light, need something from human beings. They get their strength and courage and light from the prayers of we who are here, on this side. That is why we grieve when someone dies. We think we grieve because our loved ones are gone, because we have forgotten where they have gone to. But in truth, our grief is the pain that helps us to remember them. So we think of that person, alone and lonely, and we remember their lives, things about them, with love in our hearts. That love radiates like food to the blue flames and they translate it into living rays that heal the person until he can see his angel's light and can go on into the next stage of his life.

Once I had grasped this, I began to pray for the dead, not specifically, but for all those who cross in ignorance or in knowledge. And I feel the garden within me and around me. I see nature, particularly the birds and trees, in a different way. The movement of birds, whether perched or in flight, mimics the winged motion of the light beings when they surge forth in joy at receiving us from across the river. Trees bend their branches in the wind like we move our beings in the breath of the streaming light on the other side. Our understanding of the language of angels is like the bending of trees before a storm. The wind feels more alive, flowers are fresher, and so the living garden fills my earthly home. It is, after all, one and the same, though the fact of my material body prevents me from completely seeing this all the time. 'In the midst of life, we are in death' is an actual fact. However, death is not the end. It is the beginning.

Understanding the Role of the Beasts

Another mystery has also become clear now. The beasts that we sometimes see when in meditation, as one tries to cross over, are tied directly to our having a material body. They are figments of the darkness of thinking, feeling and will when it is buried in our human material existence. The reddish one is undelivered, unredeemed actions that have led to poor fruition through their unfulfilled intentions or selfish deeds. The bluish, dirty grey beast is dead thinking come to destructive life. Meeting that beast kills all joy and life in the heart and soul. The yellowish, misshapen dog is slothful, cold feeling, that doesn't care enough and turns a blind eye to human suffering and pain. They tie us to the earth and make us blind to life beyond the river. When we die, we no longer meet them, because we have left our materialistic thinking, feeling and will behind with our body.

The forces of soul that lead us towards love are in themselves pure. They are our aspiration towards life and conquering love. But as soon as we have bodies, the darkness of matter preys on them and pulls them down. So we have to look upon the beasts as representatives of our blindness. They act as guardians of the river between this life and the life beyond, as long as we have bodies. Once we cross the river, which shrinks to nothing, firming the ground under our feet as we step over, we have left

our bodies and the beasts where they belong, here on earth —
unless, of course, like the doctor, we choose to swim in the water
of life and death!

Orientating After Death

We see, when we die, what we expect to see. If I die expecting a
black hole of nothing, this is what I will find. And the blue flame,
unseen by me and sent by my angel, will take me to the cave
where I will be healed in order to know life. If I expect a cricket
pitch, because the shock of my death is so sudden that I cannot
believe it, I will be on that cricket pitch, a place so familiar to me
that I can have time to orientate into my new state of being. And
someone whom I can recognize will greet me, explain to me
what has happened, and take me to my angel.

Most of the people that I saw arrived on the other side very
much younger than in this life. And most of them seemed happy,
even glowing with health and vitality. I was able to pick out their
clothing quite particularly, right down to their shoes and lipstick. The Queen Mother even had her handbag! Could it be
that, just as we see what is familiar to us when we first cross over
(so that we will 'feel at home' until we know better), we find
ourselves in forms closest to the time we were happiest and most
successful in life on earth?

We seem to get younger whilst we wait at the river for the
moment of crossing. There too, from being clothed all in darkness, colours already begin to appear. Are these the colours of
the soul beginning to be revealed as the body loosens its hold?
My mother and my mother-in-law wore pearl-grey dresses. Both
of them spent their lives working on inner discipline and
sharpening their skills to hear the voice of conscience. Could
different coloured clothing on the other side be related to
various soul qualities cultivated during one's life on earth? Also

the shoes of all those whom I saw were so outstandingly clear, different in style, and they seemed to impress themselves into my consciousness. Perhaps they tell of the way a person walked on the earth, their deeds and standing in relation to their spiritual endeavours.

The terrible jig that I saw some having to dance is the terrible agony of sloughing off one's attachment to the material body. We love our bodies, often fully identifying with them, and the fear of not having one fills us with terror. But death is shedding that skin, the body, and for many this is more painful than losing consciousness is for others. They have to 'dance' themselves out. I believe this is why I saw these people as black, without any relieving colour whatsoever. And yet we have form on the other side, clearly defined and heavier than that of the angels, who also have human-like forms. Angels are much bigger, higher, wider and fuller. Their livingness moves so much faster, breathed lightness that radiates and pulsates to inaudible golden sound. There seems to be a difference between our *material* and our *physical* bodies. It is as though the physical form is filled out with matter when we are here on this side, and it is this that looks black to the seeing eye, thickened and dark. Once this is sloughed off, the clearly beautiful and living physical form can be seen and inhabited much more happily.

Clearly, however, we shed this form too, at some later stage, because the struggle which the man had to appear visibly recognizable to the woman in the chair, whose link to him called him back, was his attempt to clothe himself once again in his physical existence. He had to draw himself in, narrow himself down, shape himself into a defined space within time, which seemed to be very difficult. Moreover, he came from very far away, not in space but in dimension, as though he had been dispersed into a much greater and wider sphere of beinghood.

Why We Should Pray for the Dead

I now know what my mother's death has taught me. Recently, an old man with Down's syndrome came walking down the road. We have known each other for a very long time. He is the same age as me. I went to meet him, because I had just heard that his mother, aged 91 years, had died that morning. He smiled as we met and I said: 'I hear your mother has died. How wonderful that she is now with the angels!'

He smiled broadly and answered: 'Yes! And you are next.'

I felt a flash of shock, and then I joined his laughter, grinning to myself as we parted. There is a saying: *Live each day as though it were your last.*

That afternoon, as is our custom in our community, we met in the chapel to say a prayer for the dead. We do this on the day someone has died, sometimes meeting for three successive days to read for them. We stood in a circle — only a few people, because not many of us had known his mother. And then we realized that no one had the verse by Rudolf Steiner that we usually read.* As I knew it by heart, I volunteered to say it.

> Spirits ever watchful,
> Guardians of your souls,
> May your pinions carry
> Our soul's petitioning love,
> To the human beings in the spheres
> Committed to your care,
> That united with your power,
> Our prayer may radiate with help
> To the soul whom our love is seeking.

---

* To be found in *Verses and Meditations* (Rudolf Steiner Press, London).

Once more I stood in the garden, the old lady standing shyly and humbly, her hands joined behind her back, a beaming smile on her face, wearing a dark grey suit and a necklace of pearls, talking eagerly with her own bright light-being. Over in the distance a glowing radiance from the mouth of the cave called to me and, as I approached it, this time without needing to be compelled, I saw how the blue flames shone brighter and more bravely as they went about their healing work. The red embers glowed with greater warmth, and the caskets resting there seemed less hardened and austere.

It matters so much that we know of the other side and its reality. It matters so that our prayers can sustain the blue flames of healing. It matters so that the possibility exists for some human beings to become a 'bridge' for the dying. How the living accompany the dying helps the dying to go on living. They may need an adjustment period in the cave or help from a friend who has already made the crossing. But, more than all these aids, they need the understanding and breadth of soul of those who remain here on this side. It helps them to find the light by our knowing that the light is waiting for them. They do not need to dance the jig of material death. They can walk that path to the river without so much toil and pain. Certainly, their earthly pain may be terrible, but as my mother said: 'One must die of something! It is merely a question of what will help us to cross over.' But they need not suffer the soul-pain of blackness and blindness, of a dark pit filled with flies, though I know from my mother's suffering that this also may be necessary.

The illness that causes death is the means that softens our hardened bodies so that we can finally slip out of them, as the doctor did when she put on her swim suit and dived into the waters. Pain brings consciousness, hard though it is. I do not relish what may be waiting for me when my time comes to make the final journey. But I know the light is there, as are the blue flames, ready to help me.

Life Within Life Within Life

Just as the blue flames heal us into awakening to the light beings, so the light beings, our own guardian angels, help us on the next part of the journey into life. I have not been able to go further than the first stage, but I know there is a great deal beyond the ocean of light – or possibly within it. There seems to be life within life within life, rather than beyond, as time is not an issue over there. All is simultaneity, and space is the yardstick by which we measure existence over there. So we go within, rather than onward. However, within seems to be a widening of existence, rather than a narrowing to a point, as it would be here on this side.

It is true that angels and humans work together. They cannot approach us unless we meet them half way. They understand the living quality of things and thoughts and feelings. They cannot understand the materialness of earth as we humans can. But our material understanding has caught us in the trap of thinking that that is all there is. The angels are thus shut out of our lives, and we sink into darkness and imagine the other side to be non-existent. Those who do so spend a very long time in the cave of healing blue light. Those who actively deny the light are those who lie in the warm red embers in the cave, soaking up the life that they have deliberately stifled whilst living on earth.

However, most of us at least hope that there is life after death, and we imagine it in some picture or another. The pictures we live by here will be the reality we find on the other side. The angels will slowly bring us to see the actual reality. Accompanying a loved one on their journey to death is the greatest gift that can be given. Their soul and spirit experience the crossing and one can be allowed to share with them life's greatest adventure.

All that I have tried to describe has had to take on worldly pictures. It is impossible to describe the other side in a language of light and sound and colour because the words don't exist in our material world. So I have used human language as best as I can. The path to dying from our perspective on earth may be hard and cold, or sudden and unexpected. But knowing of the light into which we die, of the life that is on the other side, is the joy of finding gold.

POSTSCRIPT

February, a year later

The book is finished. It is six o'clock, the light just fading from day into night. I sit outside on the bench under my mother's window and think back over the year, so full of changes. I hope I have succeeded in writing down the events correctly, and that what I have written will find resonance in others whose companions have crossed over the deep, dark slow river at the top of the mountain. I hope that they will recognize some parts of the picture, which I am sure everyone has caught glimpses of. I am not the only one who has seen the other side, has been able to know angels, and share insights with people who have died. I hope this account will comfort and heal those who find death such a definite parting of the ways, and that it might serve as an affirmation for those who have had similar experiences but dismissed them as the product of madness, illusion or unhinged grieving — as our materialistic age would have us think.

The mist has come down, the weathermen say it will turn to freezing fog. I look at the sandthorn tree, hazy and mysterious, at the half moon, high in the east, shedding a silver gleam on the spiky branches. The air is quite still.

Suddenly, I hear the thudding wings of geese honking loudly in the mist, invisibly flying by above the thorny tree. The sound is so clear and loud that I count seven different calls. Their wings beat the air, stirring it up, and swirling the mist overhead. The sound is awe-inspiring, louder and stronger than any other flock of geese I have witnessed before. I think it must be the silence of the mist that magnifies the sound. But I cannot see them as they swoop by. Then a lonely honk swirls above my head, the wings clearly and rhythmically beating the water droplets in the air. The geese, I think, are flying again, this time from east to west! And the single one comes last, calling out its message.

It is like a blessing; nature and the living garden are united once more. I am inwardly jubilant and satisfied.

Next morning, I sit again on the bench (since my mother's passing, I now do my meditation outside). As I sit, over the house wing two magnificent swans, calling to each other as they fly from west to east. At the sound of their mighty wings rushing over the sky, I realize that last night's visitation was not geese but a flock of those royal white birds, the swan.

MORE BOOKS ON SPIRITUAL EXPERIENCE
FROM CLAIRVIEW

www.clairviewbooks.com

AND THE WOLVES HOWLED
Fragments of two lifetimes
Barbro Karlén
ISBN 1 902636 18 X

LIGHT BEYOND THE DARKNESS
How I healed my suicide son after his death
Doré Deverell
ISBN 1 902636 19 8

LIVING WITH INVISIBLE PEOPLE
A Karmic Autobiography
Jostein Saether
ISBN 1 902636 26 0

A MESSAGE FOR HUMANITY
The Call of God's Angels at a Time of Global Crisis
K. Martin-Kuri
ISBN 1 902636 27 9

MY DESCENT INTO DEATH
and the message of love which brought me back
Howard Storm
ISBN 1 902636 16 3

PSYCHIC QUEST
Episodes from the Life of a Ghost Hunter
Natalie Osborne-Thomason
ISBN 1 902636 34 1

PSYCHIC WARRIOR
The true story of the CIA's paranormal espionage programme
David Morehouse
ISBN 1 902636 20 1

SEVEN STEPS TO ETERNITY
The true story of one man's journey into the afterlife
as told to 'psychic surgeon' Stephen Turoff
ISBN 1 902636 17 1

WHAT'S BEYOND THAT STAR
A Chronicle of Geomythic Adventure
Richard Leviton
ISBN 1 902636 32 5

WHEN THE STORM COMES
and A MOMENT IN THE BLOSSOM KINGDOM
Barbro Karlén
ISBN 1 902636 23 6

www.clairviewbooks.com